MW00396823

LEVEL

3

Jacob's Ladder

READING COMPREHENSION PROGRAM

Grades 5–6

LEVEL

3

Jacob's Ladder
READING COMPREHENSION PROGRAM
Grades 5–6

(Second Edition)

EDITED BY:
JOYCE VANTASSEL-BASKA
TAMRA STAMBAUGH

Center for Gifted Education,
The College of William and Mary

**Contributing Authors
(in alphabetical order):**
Heather French
Paula Ginsburgh
Tamra Stambaugh
Joyce VanTassel-Baska

Special Acknowledgements:
Kathryn Holt

**Funded by the United States Department of
Education, Javits Program**

PRUFROCK PRESS INC.
WACO, TEXAS

Copyright ©2009 Center for Gifted Education, The College of William and Mary

Edited by Lacy Compton
Production Design by Marjorie Parker

ISBN-13: 978-1-59363-352-3
ISBN-10: 1-59363-352-1

The purchase of this book entitles the buyer to reproduce student activity pages for classroom use only. Other use requires written permission of publisher. All rights reserved.

At the time of this book's publication, all facts and figures cited are the most current available; all telephone numbers, addresses, and Web site URLs are accurate and active; all publications, organizations, Web sites, and other resources exist as described in this book; and all have been verified. The authors and Prufrock Press make no warranty or guarantee concerning the information and materials given out by organizations or content found at Web sites, and we are not responsible for any changes that occur after this book's publication. If you find an error or believe that a resource listed here is not as described, please contact Prufrock Press.

Prufrock Press Inc.
P.O. Box 8813
Waco, TX 76714-8813
Phone: (800) 998-2208
Fax: (800) 240-0333
http://www.prufrock.com

Contents

Part I: Teachers' Guide to Jacob's Ladder Reading Comprehension Program

Introduction to *Jacob's Ladder, Level 3*

Jacob's Ladder, Level 3 is a supplemental reading program that implements targeted readings from short stories, poetry, and nonfiction sources. With this program, students engage in an inquiry process that moves from lower order to higher order thinking skills. Starting with basic literary understanding, students learn to critically analyze texts by determining implications and consequences, generalizations, main ideas, and/or creative synthesis. Suggested for students in grades 5 and 6 to enhance reading comprehension and critical thinking, *Jacob's Ladder, Level 3* tasks are organized into four skill ladders: A–D. Each ladder focuses on a different skill. Students "climb" each ladder by answering lower level questions before moving to higher level questions or rungs at the top of each ladder. Each ladder stands alone and focuses on a separate critical thinking component in reading.

Ladder A focuses on implications and consequences. By leading students through sequencing and cause and effect activities, students learn to draw implications and consequences from readings. Ladder B focuses on making generalizations. Students first learn to provide details and examples, then move to classifying and organizing those details in order to make generalizations. Ladder C focuses on themes. Students begin by identifying setting and characters and then make inferences about the literary situation. Ladder D focuses on creative synthesis by leading students through paraphrasing and summarizing activities. Table 1 provides a visual representation of the four ladders and corresponding objectives for each ladder and rung.

TABLE 1
Goals and Objectives of *Jacob's Ladder* by Ladder and Rung

A3: Consequences and Implications	B3: Generalizations	C3: Theme/Concept	D3: Creative Synthesis
Students will be able to predict character actions, story outcomes, and make real-world forecasts.	Students will be able to make general statements about a reading and/or an idea within the reading, using data to support their statements.	Students will be able to identify a major idea or theme common throughout the text.	Students will create something new using what they have learned from the reading and their synopses.
A2: Cause and Effect	**B2: Classifications**	**C2: Inference**	**D2: Summarizing**
Students will be able to identify and predict relationships between character behavior and story events, and their effects upon other characters or events.	Students will be able to categorize different aspects of the text or identify and sort categories from a list of topics or details.	Students will be able to use textual clues to read between the lines and make judgments about specific textual events, ideas, or character analysis.	Students will be able to provide a synopsis of text sections.
A1: Sequencing	**B1: Details**	**C1: Literary Elements**	**D1: Paraphrasing**
Students will be able to list, in order of importance or occurrence in the text, specific events or plot summaries.	Students will be able to list specific details or recall facts related to the text or generate a list of ideas about a specific topic or character.	Students will be able to identify and explain specific story elements such as character, setting, or poetic device.	Students will be able to restate lines read using their own words.
Ladder A	Ladder B	Ladder C	Ladder D

The *Jacob's Ladder* series consists of seven levels: Primary 1, Primary 2, and Levels 1–5. Levels 1–5 contain short stories, poetry, and nonfiction selections including biography, as well as at least two commensurate ladders for each selection, with the exception of Primary 1 poetry, which has one ladder per poem. *Jacob's Ladder Primary 1* and *Primary 2* differ from the rest of the series in that the majority of the short stories are Caldecott Medal or Caldecott Honor picture books. Many of the stories are intended to be read aloud for the first reading. In addition, although *Jacob's Ladder Primary 1* does contain poetry, it does not contain nonfiction selections.

Jacob's Ladder Primary 1 is recommended for gifted readers in grades K–1, *Jacob's Ladder Primary 2* is recommended for gifted readers in grades 1–2, *Jacob's Ladder Level 1* is recommended for bright students in grades 2–3, *Jacob's Ladder Level 2* is recommended for students in grades 4–5, and *Jacob's Ladder Level 3* is recommended for students in grades 5–6. *Jacob's Ladder Level 4* and *Level 5* are recommended for middle and early high school students in grades 7–9. However, teachers may find that they want to vary usage beyond the recommended levels, depending on student abilities. Evidence suggests that the curriculum can be successfully implemented with gifted learners and advanced readers, as well as promising learners, at different grade levels. Thus, the levels vary and overlap to provide opportunities for teachers to select the most appropriate set of readings for meaningful differentiation for their gifted, bright, or promising learners.

Ladder A:
Focus on Implications and Consequences

The goal of Ladder A is to develop prediction and forecasting skills by encouraging students to make connections among the information provided. Starting with sequencing, students learn to recognize basic types of change that occur within a text. Through identifying cause and effect relationships, students then can judge the impact of certain events. Finally, through recognizing consequences and implications, students predict future events as logical and identify both short- and long-term consequences by judging probable outcomes based on data provided. The rungs are as follows:

- **Ladder A, Rung 1, Sequencing**: The lowest rung on the ladder, sequencing, requires students to organize a set of information in order, based on their reading (e.g., List the steps of a recipe in order).

- **Ladder A, Rung 2, Cause and Effect**: The middle rung, cause and effect, requires students to think about relationships and identify what causes certain effects and/or what effects were brought about because of certain causes (e.g., What causes a cake to rise in the oven? What effect does the addition of egg yolks have on a batter?).

- **Ladder A, Rung 3, Consequences and Implications**: The highest rung on Ladder A requires students to think about both short-term and long-term events that may happen as a result of an effect they have identified (e.g., What are the short-term and long-term consequences of baking at home?). Students learn to draw consequences and implications from text for application in the real world.

Ladder B: Focus on Generalizations

The goal of Ladder B is to help students develop deductive reasoning skills, moving from the concrete elements in a story to abstract ideas. Students begin by learning the importance of concrete details and how they can be organized. By the top rung, students are able to make general statements spanning a topic or concept. The rungs are as follows:

- **Ladder B, Rung 1, Details**: The lowest rung on Ladder B, details/examples, requires students to list examples or details from what they have read and/or to list examples they know from the real world or have read about (e.g., Make a list of examples of transportation. Write as many as you can think of in 2 minutes).

- **Ladder B, Rung 2, Classifications**: The middle rung of Ladder B focuses on students' ability to categorize examples and details based on characteristics (e.g., How might we categorize the modes of transportation you identified?). This activity builds students' skills in categorization and classification.

- **Ladder B, Rung 3, Generalizations**: The highest rung on Ladder B, generalization, requires students to use the list and categories generated at Rungs 1 and 2 to develop 2–3 general statements that apply to *all* of their examples (e.g., Write three statements about transportation).

Ladder C: Focus on Themes

The goal of Ladder C is to develop literary analysis skills based on an understanding of literary elements. After completing Ladder C, students state main themes and ideas of text after identifying setting, characters, and the context of the piece. The rungs are as follows:

- **Ladder C, Rung 1, Literary Elements**: While working on Rung 1, students identify and/or describe the setting or situation in which the reading occurs. This rung also requires students to develop an understanding of given characters by identifying qualities he or she possesses and comparing these qualities to other characters they have encountered in their reading (e.g., In *Goldilocks and the Three Bears*, what is the situation in which Goldilocks finds herself? What qualities do you admire in Goldilocks? What qualities do you find problematic? How is she similar or different from other fairy tale characters you have encountered?).

- **Ladder C, Rung 2, Inference**: Inference serves as the middle rung of this ladder and requires students to think through a situation in the text and come to a conclusion based on the information and clues provided (e.g., What evidence exists that Goldilocks ate the porridge? What inferences can you make about the bear's subsequent action?).

- **Ladder C, Rung 3, Theme/Concept**: As the highest rung of Ladder C, this step requires students to state the central idea or theme for a reading. This exercise asks students to explain an idea from the reading that best states what the text means (e.g., How would you rename the fairy tale? Why? What is the overall theme of *Goldilocks and the Three Bears*? Which of the following morals apply to the fairy tale? Why or why not?).

Ladder D: Focus on Creative Synthesis

The goal of Ladder D is to help students develop skills in creative synthesis in order to foster students' creation of new material based on information from the reading. It moves from the level of restating ideas to creating new ideas about a topic or concept. The rungs are as follows:

- **Ladder D, Rung 1, Paraphrasing**: The lowest rung on Ladder D is paraphrasing. This rung requires students to restate a short passage using their own words (e.g., Rewrite the following quotation in your own words: "But as soon as [the slave] came near to Androcles, he recognized his friend, and fawned upon him, and licked his hands like a friendly dog. The emperor, surprised at this, summoned Androcles to him, who told the whole story. Whereupon the slave was pardoned and freed, and the Lion let loose to his native forest.").

- **Ladder D, Rung 2, Summarizing**: Summarizing, the middle rung, requires students to summarize larger sections of text by selecting the most important key points within a passage (e.g., Choose one section of the story and summarize it in five sentences).

- **Ladder D, Rung 3, Creative Synthesis**: The highest rung on Ladder D requires students to create something new using what they have learned from the reading and their synopses of it (e.g., Write another fable about the main idea you identified for this fable, using characters, setting, and a plot of your choice).

Process Skills

Along with the four goals addressed by the ladders, a fifth goal, process skills, is incorporated in the *Jacob's Ladder* curriculum. The aim of this goal is to promote learning through interaction and discussion of reading material in the classroom. After completing the ladders and following guidelines for discussion and teacher feedback, students will be able to:

- articulate their understanding of a reading passage using textual support,
- engage in proper dialogue about the meaning of a selection, and
- discuss varied ideas about intention of a passage both orally and in writing.

Reading Genres and Selections

The reading selections include three major genres: short stories (fables, myths, short stories, and essays), poetry, and nonfiction. In Level 3, each reading within a genre has been carefully selected or tailored for fifth-grade reading accessibility and interest. The stories and poems for the *Jacob's Ladder* curriculum at each grade level were chosen with three basic criteria in mind: (1) concrete to abstract development, (2) level of vocabulary, and (3) age-appropriate themes. The readings and exercises are designed to move students forward in their abstract thinking processes by promoting critical and creative thinking. The vocabulary in each reading is grade-level appropriate, however when new or unfamiliar words are encountered, they should be covered in class before readings and ladder questions are assigned. Themes also are appropriate to the students' ages at each grade level and were chosen to complement themes typically seen in texts for each particular level. The short stories, poetry, and nonfiction readings with corresponding ladder sets are delineated in Part II. Table 2 outlines all Level 3 readings by genre.

TABLE 2
Reading Selections by Genre

Fables/Myths/Short Stories/Essays	Poetry	Nonfiction
Brazilian Paradise	A Corn Song	Economics 101
Christa McAuliffe: A Teacher on Earth and in Space!	The Harp	Mass, Volume, and Density
The Competition	I Am the Moon	Population Explosion: How Math Helps You Understand America's Past
Excerpts From Common Sense	If	The Systems of the Human Body: Part I
Franklin D. Roosevelt's First Inaugural Address	The Lament of the Frog Prince	The Systems of the Human Body: Part II
The Gettysburg Address	The Road Not Taken	What Is Sound?
Legacy	Sinking Sunset	
Moving Pictures Evoke Concern, 1922	Sunset	
Washington's Letter to His Wife Martha	The Visit	
Why Own a House When You Can Own an R.V.?	A Winter Morning	

Rationale

Constructing meaning of the written word is one of the earliest tasks required of students in schools. This skill occupies the central place in the curriculum at the elementary level. Yet, approaches to teaching reading comprehension often are "skill and drill," using worksheets on low-level reading material. As a result, students frequently are unable to transfer these skills from exercise pages and apply them to new higher level reading material.

The time expended to ensure that students become autonomous and advanced readers would suggest the need for a methodology that deliberately moves students from simple to complex reading skills with grade-appropriate texts. Such a learning approach to reading skill development ensures that students can traverse easily from basic comprehension skills to higher level critical reading skills, while using the same reading stimulus to navigate this transition. Reading comprehension is enhanced by instructional scaffolding, moving students from lower order to higher order thinking, using strategies and processes to help students analyze passages (Fielding & Pearson, 1994; Villaume & Brabham, 2002). In addition, teachers who emphasize higher order thinking through questions and tasks such as those at the higher rungs of each ladder promote greater reading growth (Knapp et al., 1995; Taylor, Pearson, Peterson, & Rodriguez, 2003).

Jacob's Ladder was written in response to teacher findings that students needed additional scaffolding to consistently work at higher levels of thinking in reading. In addition, an analysis of reading reform curriculum by the American Federation of Teachers (AFT, 1998) shows that only two of the recommended curricula posit a research base and a focus on critical thinking skills in reading. Similarly, Tivnan and Hemphill (2005) studied reading reform curricula in Title I schools and found that none of the reading programs studied emphasized skills beyond basic phonemic awareness, fluency, or limited comprehension. Therefore, supplementary curriculum that focuses on higher level thinking skills is needed.

The *Jacob's Ladder* program is a compilation of the instructional scaffolding and reading exercises necessary to aid students in their journey toward becoming critical readers. Students learn concept development skills through learning to generalize, predicting and forecasting skills through delineating implications of events, and literary analysis skills through discerning textual meaning. The questions and tasks for each reading are open-ended, as this type of approach to responding to literature improves performance on comprehension tests (Guthrie, Schafer, & Huang, 2001). Progressing through the hierarchy of skills also requires students to reread the text, thereby improving metacomprehension accuracy (Rawson, Dunlosky, & Thiede, 2000).

Research Base

A quasi-experimental study was conducted using *Jacob's Ladder* as a supplementary program for students in Title I schools, grades 3–5. After professional development occurred, experimental teachers were instructed to implement the *Jacob's Ladder* curriculum in addition to their basal reading series and guided reading groups. Teachers in the control group taught their district-adopted textbook reading series as the main curriculum.

Findings from this study ($N = 495$) suggest that when compared to students who used the basal reader only, those students who were exposed to the *Jacob's Ladder* curriculum showed significant gains in reading comprehension and critical thinking. Likewise, students who used the curriculum showed significant and important growth on curriculum-based assessments that included determining implications/consequences, making inferences, outlining themes and generalizations, and applying creative synthesis. Students reported greater interest in reading and eluded that the curriculum made them "think harder." Teachers reported more in-depth student discussion and personal growth in the ability to ask open-ended questions when reading (Stambaugh, 2008).

Implementation Considerations

Teachers need to consider certain issues when implementing the *Jacob's Ladder* curriculum. Although the program is targeted for promising students who need more exposure to higher level thinking skills in reading, the program may be suitable for learners who are functioning above or below grade level.

As modeling, coaching, and feedback appear to enhance student growth in reading and writing (Pressley et al., 2001; Taylor, Peterson, Pearson, & Rodriguez, 2002), it is recommended that teachers review how to complete the task ladders with the entire class at least once, outlining expectations and record-keeping tasks, as well as modeling the process prior to assigning small-group or independent work. Students should complete the ladder tasks on their own paper or on the template provided in Appendix B. As students gain more confidence in the curriculum, the teacher should allow more independent work coupled with small group or paired discussion, and then whole-group sharing with teacher feedback.

Completing these activities in dyads or small groups will facilitate discussions that stress collaborative reasoning, thereby fostering greater engagement and higher level thinking (Chin, Anderson, & Waggoner, 2001; Pressley et al., 2001; Taylor et al., 2002). The stories and accompanying ladder questions and activities also may be organized into a reading center in the classroom or utilized with reading groups during guided reading.

Process of *Jacob's Ladder*

The process of inquiry and feedback, as led and modeled by the teacher, is critical to the success of the program and student mastery of process skills. Teachers need to encourage and solicit multiple student responses and encourage dialogue about various perspectives and interpretations of a given text, requiring students to justify their answers with textual support and concrete examples. Student use of the ladders depends on teacher stance and modeling as well as student readiness. After teacher modeling, students should understand how to use the ladders as prescribed by the teacher. Sample follow-up questions such as those listed below can be used by the teacher and posted in the classroom to help guide student discussion.

- That's interesting; does anyone have a different idea?

- What in the story makes you say that?

- What do you think the author means by . . . ?

- What do you think are the implications or consequences to . . . ?
- Did anyone view that differently? How?
- Does anyone have a different point of view? Justify your answer.
- In the story I noticed that . . . Do you think that might have significance to the overall meaning?
- I heard someone say that he thought the poem (story) was about . . . What do you think? Justify your answer from the events of the story.
- Do you notice any key words that might be significant? Why?
- Do you notice any words that give you a mental picture? Do those words have significance? What might they symbolize?
- I agree with . . . because
- I had a different idea than . . . because

Grouping Students

Jacob's Ladder may be used in a number of different grouping patterns. The program should be introduced initially as a whole-group activity directed by the teacher with appropriate open-ended questions, feedback, and monitoring. After students have examined each type of ladder with teacher guidance, they should be encouraged to use the program by writing ideas independently, sharing with a partner, and then discussing the findings with a group. The dyad approach provides maximal opportunities for student discussion of the readings and collaborative decisions about the answers to questions posed. One purpose of the program is to solicit meaningful discussion of the text. Like-ability groups are recommended (Kulik & Kulik, 1992) for discussion.

Pre- and Postassessments and Grading

The pre- and postassessments included in Appendix A were designed as a diagnostic-prescriptive approach to guide program implementation prior to the implementation of *Jacob's Ladder*. The pretest should be administered, scored, and then used to guide student instruction and the selection of readings for varied ability groups. Both the pre- and postassessment, scoring rubric, and sample exemplars for each rubric category and level are included in Appendix A along with exemplars to guide scoring.

In both the pre- and postassessments, students read a short passage and respond to the four questions. Question 1 focuses on implications and consequences (Ladder A); Question 2 on generalization, theme, and concept (Ladders B and C); Question 3 on inference (Ladder C); and Question 4 on creative synthesis (Ladder D). By analyzing each question and scored response, teachers may wish to guide reading selections toward the appropriate ladders and stories based on student need.

Upon conclusion of the program or as a midpoint check, the posttest may be administered to compare the pretest results and to measure growth in students' responses. These pre/post results could be used as part of a student portfolio, in a parent-teacher conference, or documentation of curriculum effectiveness and student progress. The pre- and postassessments were piloted to ensure that both forms were equivalent in difficulty ($\alpha = .76$) and that the interrater reliability of scorers was appropriate ($\alpha = .81$).

Student Reflection, Feedback, and Record Keeping

Students may use an answer sheet such as the one provided in Appendix B for each ladder to record their personal thoughts independently before discussing with a partner. After finishing both of the ladders for each reading selection, a reflection page (also in Appendix B) can be provided, indicating the student's personal assessment of the work completed. Teachers also will want to check student answers as ladder segments are completed and conduct an error analysis. Individual or small-group consultation should occur at this time to ensure that students understand what they did incorrectly and why. In order to analyze student responses and progress across the program, teachers need to monitor student performance, using the student answer sheets to indicate appropriate completion of tasks. Specific comments about student work also are important to promote growth and understanding of content.

Record-keeping sheets for the class also are provided in Appendix B. On these forms, teachers record student progress on a 3-point scale: 2 (*applies skills very effectively*), 1 (*understands and applies skills*), or a 0 (*needs more practice with the given skill set*) across readings and ladder sets. This form can be used as part of a diagnostic-prescriptive approach to selecting reading materials and ladders based on student understanding or the need for more practice.

Sample Concluding Activities

Grading the ladders and responses are at the teacher's discretion. Teachers should not overemphasize the lower rungs in graded activities. Lower rungs are intended only as a vehicle to the higher level questions at the top of the ladder. Instead, top rung questions may be used as a journal prompt or as part of a graded open-ended writing response. Grades also could be given based on guided discussion after students are trained on appropriate ways to discuss literature. Additional ideas for grading are as follows:

- Write a persuasive essay to justify what you think the story is about.

- Create a symbol to show the meaning of the story. Write two sentences to justify your answer.

- In one word or phrase, what is this story mostly about? Justify your answer using examples from the story.

- Write a letter from the author's point of view, explaining what the meaning of the story is to young children.

- Pretend you are an illustrator. Create a drawing for the story or poem that shows the main idea or theme. Write a sentence that describes your illustration and theme.

Time Allotment

Although the time needed to complete *Jacob's Ladder* tasks will vary by student, most ladders should take students 15 minutes to read the selection and another 15–20 minutes to complete one ladder individually. More time is required for paired student and whole-group discussion of the questions. Teachers may wish to set aside 2 days each week for focusing on one *Jacob's Ladder* reading and the two commensurate ladders, especially when introducing the program.

Answer Key

An answer key is included at the end of the book. It contains a set of suggested answers for all questions related to each reading selection. All of the questions are somewhat open-ended; therefore, answers may vary.

The answers provided in the key are simply suggestions to help illustrate the skills targeted by each ladder skill set.

Alignment to Standards

Tables 3, 4, and 5 contain alignment charts to demonstrate the connection of the fiction and nonfiction reading materials to relevant national standards in all subject areas. One of the benefits of this program is its ability to provide cross-disciplinary coverage of standards through the use of a single reading stimulus.

TABLE 3
Standards Alignment: Short Stories

Language Arts—Short Stories	Brazilian Paradise	Christa McAuliffe: A Teacher on Earth and in Space!	The Competition	Excerpts From Common Sense	Franklin D. Roosevelt's First Inaugural Address	The Gettysburg Address	Legacy	Moving Pictures Evoke Concern, 1922	Washington's Letter to His Wife Martha	Why Own a House When You Can Own an R.V.?
The student will use analysis of text, including the interaction of the text with reader's feelings and attitudes to create response.	✗	✗		✗					✗	✗
The student will interpret and analyze the meaning of literary works from diverse cultures and authors by applying different critical lenses and analytic techniques.	✗	✗	✗	✗	✗	✗	✗	✗	✗	✗
The student will integrate various cues and strategies to comprehend what he or she reads.	✗	✗	✗	✗	✗	✗	✗	✗	✗	✗
The student will use knowledge of the purposes, structures, and elements of writing to analyze and interpret various types of text.	✗	✗	✗	✗	✗	✗	✗	✗	✗	✗
Students will use word-analysis skills, context clues, and other strategies to read fiction and nonfiction with fluency and accuracy.	✗	✗	✗	✗	✗	✗	✗	✗	✗	✗

TABLE 4
Standards Alignment: Poetry

Language Arts—Poetry	A Corn-Song	The Harp	I Am the Moon	If	The Lament of the Frog Prince	The Road Not Taken	Sinking Sunset	Sunset	The Visit	A Winter Morning
The student will use analysis of text, including the interaction of the text with reader's feelings and attitudes to create response.	✗	✗	✗	✗	✗	✗	✗	✗	✗	✗
The student will interpret and analyze the meaning of literary works from diverse cultures and authors by applying different critical lenses and analytic techniques.	✗	✗	✗	✗	✗	✗	✗	✗	✗	✗
The student will integrate various cues and strategies to comprehend what he or she reads.	✗	✗	✗	✗	✗	✗	✗	✗	✗	✗
The student will use knowledge of the purposes, structures, and elements of writing to analyze and interpret various types of text.	✗	✗	✗		✗		✗	✗		
Students will use word-analysis skills, context clues, and other strategies to read fiction and nonfiction with fluency and accuracy.										

TABLE 5
Standards Alignment: Nonfiction

Social Studies, Science, and Math Standards	Economics 101	Mass, Volume, and Density	Population Explosion: How Math Helps You Understand America's Past	Systems of the Human Body: Part I	Systems of the Human Body: Part II	What Is Sound?
Social Studies Standards						
Culture	✗					
Time, Continuity, and Change	✗		✗			
People, Places, and Environments	✗					
Individual Development and Identity						
Individuals, Groups, and Institutions	✗		✗			
Science, Technology, and Society						
Science Standards						
Science as Inquiry		✗				
Physical Science						✗
Life Science				✗	✗	
Earth and Space Science						
Science and Technology						
Science in Personal and Social Perspectives				✗	✗	
History and Nature of Science						
Math Standards						
Number and Operations	✗					
Geometry		✗				
Measurement		✗	✗			✗
Data Analysis and Probability			✗			
Problem Solving	✗	✗				
Communication						
Connections						

References

American Federation of Teachers. (1998). *Building on the best, learning from what works: Seven promising reading and English language arts programs.* Washington, DC: Author.

Chin, C. A., Anderson, R. C., & Waggoner, M. A. (2001). Patterns of discourse in two kinds of literature discussion. *Reading Research Quarterly, 36,* 378–411.

Fielding, L. G., & Pearson, P. D. (1994). Reading comprehension: What works. *Educational Leadership, 51*(5), 62–67.

Guthrie, J. T., Schafer, W. D., & Huang, C. (2001). Benefits of opportunity to read and balanced reading instruction on the NAEP. *Journal of Educational Research, 94,* 145–162.

Knapp, M. S., Adelman, N. E., Marder, C., McCollum, H., Needels, M. C., Padilla, C., et al. (1995). *Teaching for meaning in high-poverty classrooms.* New York: Teachers College Press.

Kulik, J. A., & Kulik, C. (1992). Meta-analytic findings on grouping programs. *Gifted Child Quarterly, 36,* 73–77.

Pressley, M., Wharton-McDonald, R., Allington, R., Block, C. C., Morrow, L., Tracey, D., et al. (2001). A study of effective first-grade literacy instruction. *Scientific Studies of Reading, 5,* 35–58.

Rawson, K. A., Dunlosky, J., & Thiede, K. W. (2000). The rereading effect: Metacomprehension accuracy improves across reading trials. *Memory & Cognition, 28,* 1004–1010.

Stambaugh, T. (2008). *Effects of the Jacob's Ladder Reading Comprehension Program.* Manuscript submitted for publication.

Taylor, B. M., Pearson, P. D., Peterson, D. S., & Rodriguez, M. C. (2003). Reading growth in high-poverty classrooms: The influence of teacher practices that encourage cognitive engagement in literacy learning. *The Elementary School Journal, 104,* 3–30.

Taylor, B. M., Peterson, D. S., Pearson, P. D., & Rodriguez, M. C. (2002). Looking inside classrooms: Reflecting on the "how" as well as the "what" in effective reading instruction. *Reading Teacher, 56,* 270–279.

Tivnan, T., & Hemphill, L. (2005). Comparing four literacy reform models in high-poverty schools: Patterns of first grade achievement. *Elementary School Journal, 105,* 419–443.

Villaume, S. K., & Brabham, E. G. (2002). Comprehension instruction: Beyond strategies. *The Reading Teacher, 55,* 672–676.

Part II: Readings and Student Ladder Sets

CHAPTER 1

Short Stories

Chapter 1 includes the selected readings and accompanying question sets for each short story selection. Each reading is followed by one or two sets of questions; each set is aligned to one of the four ladder skills.

For *Jacob's Ladder 3*, the skills covered by each selection are as follows:

Brazilian Paradise

A Memoir

Lush fruit trees release a delicious fragrance that mingles with the moist smell of flowers and fresh air. Behind it, a sunset of more colors than a painting glitters on the horizon. A shimmering lake reflects the sun as it sinks in the sky. Snowy egrets fly over and echo their voices across the water as they swoop down to pick up fish. This is the closest I've come to paradise.

Before I came to Brazil, I liked nature, as much as the average 9-year-old did. Trees were cool, monkeys were definitely cool . . . but that was as far as it went.

My dad is a Foreign Service Officer so we have traveled all around the world. After I finished third grade, we set off to live in Brazil for 3 years, my second experience living in a foreign country, as I lived in Moscow, Russia, as a toddler.

My first experiences with Brazilian nature weren't very interesting at all. We started out living in an old apartment building in a commercial area. The building was surrounded by strips of stores, roads, other apartment buildings, and a little bit of nature—red dirt and patches of dry grass. When we finally got to our house, things began to change.

Our house was surrounded by tall palm trees, colorful flowering trees, and had a huge, spellbinding backyard. The yard went back from our house fairly far and the end was a forest of tropical trees. All sorts of fruit trees grew there and vines crept up the walls of our large home.

Bird songs crowded the air from well before dawn to well after dusk. In the grasses of our yard, if I looked closely, I could see a moving trail of leaves passing by. It would make anyone do a double take, at first sight. But sure enough, there they were . . . leaf-cutter ants marching with deep green leaves and bright flower fragments held high above their heads. You could almost hear the left-right, left-right, pit-pat, pit-pat as if the ants were tiny marching soldiers.

The day brought sweet breezes that lingered about through the night. It is a common misconception that Brazil is extremely hot, but where I lived, Brasilia, at 3,000 feet elevation, it was never too cool and, because there was no humidity, rarely too hot. Many Americans would be used to lots of gray drizzle when it rained. In Brasilia, cool rain ripped open the clouds, shattered the clear air, and drenched the thirsty earth, for a brief bit of time.

A day at a local park, halfway through my time in Brazil, brought an exciting and fantastic discovery. My parents and I were sitting in the shade by a mineral water pool where people were swimming. As we looked around, my mom's eyes fell upon a grove of trees. Suddenly, she called out in delight: "Monkeys! Emily, Greg, look!" She pointed in the direction of the trees and we jerked our heads to look.

"Where?" I cried.

Then we saw them. Gorgeous, tiny monkeys skittering about the trees. We turned our heads to find a couple of big ones, too. We scooted back and forth around the trees, awestruck by seeing wild monkeys. One little monkey scurried about a branch with a plastic water bottle and soon began banging it on the tree to try to break it open. After realizing her goal was quite impossible, the monkey flung the bottle out of the tree. Our attention soared back to the playful monkeys, or in Portuguese, "macacos," as they danced in the trees.

Soon, we discovered a whole new world of fabulous creatures. We began to see possums, anteaters, and marmosets in our yard. Each time, we would fly to the window or even outside, and watch the excitement.

Starlit nights possessed a certain magic. The Milky Way would often stand out, its mystery and wonder swallowing us. My parents used to put lawn chairs in our backyard and stare up into the vast, glittering sky. I was often chilled, despite the fact that it wasn't cold, to sit in such blackness and awe. Weekends provided free time for daddy-daughter bike rides. Our wheels would spin through our favorite (and closest) park, on a promontory by the lake, which we had appropriately named "The Point." Along the lakeshore, my dad and I often stopped by a long boat dock, which was actually part of a Brazilian Navy Admiral's property. We would sit and watch the birds fly across the sky and listen to the gentle waves, which carried stories from other shores, lap at the dock. Those were treasured moments where I slowly began to see nature in a different way. More like a spell of magic, a gift.

Many of the other employees who worked in the Embassy purchased Brazil Passes, a way to travel cheaply to more than one Brazil location in one trip. When my family purchased one of these, I had my first and only trip to the Amazon Rainforest. Discovery took place day and night as I canoed down Amazonian rivers, watched glamorous river dolphins glide through the water, saw wild macaws, and found dead piranhas on the shore or floating in the water. About 2 weeks before we left Brazil, we were at a party with some other Embassy employees, when we came across our first wild toucan. This bird represented perfectly the color and thrill of Brazilian nature. It's a deep black color with eyes as blue as the mystical skies. Its beak reflects the colors of trees, flowers, and various other things. It was a friendly, graceful, but also funny bird that was a joy to watch. After leaving Brazil, I missed the wildlife tremendously. I began to realize then, even more than ever, how truly precious nature was. The bright colors, sparkling stars, and magical moments had shown me, and I would never feel the same about wildlife again.

By Emily Thielmann
First Place: Essays, Grades 6–8
The College of William and Mary Writing Talent Search

Consequences and Implications

A3

Suppose a group of developers decides they want to increase commercialization in Brazil. What are some of the potential consequences and implications of doing so?

Cause and Effect

A2

What caused the area of Brazil where the author and her family first lived to be devoid of nature? What effects did it have?

Sequencing

A1

List the five most important events in the story in order.

BRAZILIAN PARADISE

 Jacob's Ladder Reading Comprehension Program, Level 3 © Prufrock Press • This page may be photocopied or reproduced with permission for classroom use.

Generalizations

B3

What generalizations can you make about the nature of Brazil? About nature in general?

Classifications

B2

Classify the details in your list into categories.

Details

B1

List all the details you can find that the author provides about the natural setting of Brazil.

BRAZILIAN PARADISE

Christa McAuliffe:
A Teacher on Earth and in Space!

On January 28, 1986, the world not only lost the space shuttle, Challenger, but it lost a real challenger in life, Sharon Christa McAuliffe. Christa had been selected to ride aboard the Space Shuttle Challenger as the first civilian in space. She was going to space to do what she did on Earth: teach. She was going to teach two lessons. One, she was going to give a tour of the shuttle, and two, she was going to cover the history, as well as the future, of space. Sadly, Christa never got this chance.

The space shuttle, 51-L, known as the Challenger, exploded after only 73 seconds in the air, killing all seven crew members, including Christa McAuliffe. The explosion had been caused by the failure of the primary and secondary O-rings to form an airtight seal because they were so stiff from the cold temperatures. When hot gases burned through the primary O-ring, the secondary O-ring was not in position to stop the gases from burning through the outer casing of the solid rocket booster. Fire erupted, burning the external tank and allowing fuel to spill out, igniting the Challenger and ripping it apart.

Christa's life began in August 1948. She was raised in Framingham, MA, with her two sisters, Lisa and Betsy, and her two brothers, Steven and Kit. Even as a child Christa loved to teach. At a young age she taught her brothers and sisters how to knit, bake, play the guitar, and many other things. But most importantly she taught them how to be kind and care about other things. Christa also began Girl Scouts at an early age and her love for this program carried on throughout the rest of her life. She began counseling with the Girl Scouts in high school and helped open up Camp Wabasso as an adult.

Christa was a good student, liked by everyone at Marian High School. At this high school she met her future husband, Steve McAuliffe. While Steve went to the Virginia Military Institute for college, Christa attended Framingham State College. This is where her goal to be a teacher began, majoring in history and education.

Following Christa's and Steve's graduation from college, they got married. Even then Christa was independent, making her own wedding dress. They lived in Maryland where Christa got a job teaching social studies at Thomas Jefferson Middle School from 1971–1978. In 1978 Steve and Christa moved to Concord, NH, with their two children, Caroline and Scott. There she got a job again teaching social studies at Concord High School until she died.

On July 19, 1985, Vice President George H. W. Bush announced Christa McAuliffe the winner out of 11,146 entries to be the first citizen and teacher in space. During the selection process the Teacher-in-Space nominees were required to answer a question (not known in advance) to "describe your philosophy of life." Christa answered that her philosophy of life was first to get as much out of life as possible, to be flexible, to try new things, and to connect with people. She pointed out that one reason she went into teaching was to have an impact on others and to feel that impact on herself. She often said that she learned as much from her students as she taught them. NASA professionals said she had the "right stuff" and it took them only 20 minutes to give her all seven votes. Christa was going to teach in space until tragedy happened.

Through this paper, I hope to leave with you at least a suspicion that great people are really ordinary people who try their best, who try even though they might be afraid to fail, and who, above all else, know the vital necessity for each of us to be true to ourselves.

Christa knew these things, and she acted on that knowledge. Christa was a hero, a real hero, but perhaps not for reasons that you might think.

Rather, she is not a hero because she died while seeking to expand her knowledge and to explore space. She is not a hero because she took a calculated risk as the first private citizen to venture into space. She is not a hero because she brought such needed credit to her teaching profession.

Rather, she is a hero because long before the Teacher-In-Space program was ever thought of, she overcame many of life's ordinary obstacles and became a worthy person, a person of value to herself and of value to those who shared this life with her. In short, she is a real hero because she actually did with her life what each of us is capable of doing with our own lives. Christa lived. She never sat back and just existed. Sharon Christa McAuliffe was a true hero!

Bibliography

Biel, T. L. (1990). *The Challenger*. Farmington Hills, MI: Lucent Books.

Corrigan, G. G. (1993). *A journal for Christa*. Lincoln: University of Nebraska Press.

Hamilton, S. L. (1988). *Space shuttle Challenger explosion*. Minneapolis, MN: Abdo Consulting Group.

By Caroline R. Titcomb
Second Place: Essays, Grades 6–8
The College of William and Mary Writing Talent Search

CHRISTA MCAULIFFE

Consequences and Implications

A3

How might the space exploration program be different if the Challenger mission had been successful?

Cause and Effect

A2

What caused Christa McAuliffe to want to teach in space? Support your answer.

Sequencing

A1

List the events of the Challenger accident in order.

Theme/Concept

C3

In what ways does the author address the concept of bravery?

Inference

C2

Could the Challenger accident have been avoided? How do you know? Describe the cause and effect relationship that resulted in the accident.

Literary Elements

C1

Do you think, as the author does, that Christa McAuliffe was a heroine? Why?

CHRISTA MCAULIFFE

The Competition

Slowly and carefully, I tune my violin in the solitude of the warm-up room. I play a couple of scales, run through some arpeggios, then check the clock again. Half an hour until the competition begins. Half an hour until I walk out on stage and become either the sole winner or one of the many losers. I tell myself not to think that way, just to do my best . . . yeah, right. Sure, you can say what you like but the truth is the truth: Everyone is here to win, or at least I am. The way I see it, I haven't spent 3 months preparing for this thing only to show up, bomb it, and go home empty-handed. I have resolved to win and that's that.

Now I am running through my piece, envisioning that I am on-stage and the judges are watching, keeping an eye out for any mistake, any hesitation at all. After I have played my solo three times, I check the clock again. Four more minutes and it's time to go. I close my eyes and silently run my hands over the fingerboard, carefully manipulating every phrase, revising where necessary, every note a silver inscription in my brain. Another glance at my watch tells me it's time to head for the auditorium. Gripping my violin tightly, I take a deep breath and walk out into the hall.

Someone hands me a program. Hastily I scan through the names. Good. Out of 12 performers, I am 10th on the list, near the end. Hopefully, I'll make an impression on the judges and they'll remember how I played.

The first contestant is up on the stage now, a pianist. I watch his fingers run over the keys. He is good, but I'm positive I can beat him. Confidence abounds. I want this so much that I can visualize it.

Time passes slowly as one musician performs after another. Although the audience is duly appreciative, none of them really grabs my attention. They are all good, but no one is astounding or breathtaking. Still, I am nervous. I ask myself what could possibly go wrong. When I think about it, the true answer is of course an abundance of things: anything from a simple mistake to a nosebleed. Just as I am making this list in my head, I hear the ninth musician, another pianist, begin his piece. I suddenly sit in rapt attention, adrenaline shooting through me like electricity. His performance is astonishing. When he finishes, his final beautiful, perfect note hangs suspended like a cloud over the audience. He bows with perfect grace, flashes a broad and charming grin, and leaves the stage. He thinks he has won, and to be perfectly honest, so do I. Now, I think, I have something to be nervous about. Inside my mind I hold a silent soliloquy.

The audience has settled down; it's my turn to play. I have slipped from my nervous, sweaty-palmed state into a calm, controlled, and very confident one. I am not going to let any pianist, no matter how wonderful, stand in my way of winning. My name is called, my piece introduced, and I ascend onto the stage regally, ready to win over this audience, sweep them off their feet. I take a deep breath, feeling the tense silence in the room, hundreds of eyes on me, and then I let my fingers fly.

It is golden. I nail it. In fact, I think what I have just played was absolute perfection, at least by my standards. I feel so ecstatic I cannot remember getting off stage and back to my seat. The applause is just dying down. What the judges decide is now out of my hands, but I have done my job. Now all I have to do is wait. I do not even hear the last two performers; time grinds by as if submerged in water somehow. When I shake out of this trance, I chat nervously with the performer next to me, the one who did such a miraculous job. I tell him he has amazing talent, and he returns the compliment. We both know we are each other's nemesis.

The judges are taking forever. I hear pencils scratching, papers turning over. They are comparing scores; soon they will verify the winner and I will either be ecstatic or extremely disappointed. Finally a man walks onto the stage and addresses the audience. I expect him to render the verdict, but instead he apologizes for the long wait. He says the judges have had a tough time deciding on a winner. My stomach churns through his improvised speech. I don't need an apology—I want to know the results! The man rambles on, telling us how even if the outcome is not what we expect or wish for we are all winners in the end, nobody is a loser. My palms are sweaty and slippery now, I grip the bottom of my seat. I don't need to hear this, I have heard it a million times from my parents and teachers. When he finally takes out an envelope given to him by the judges, I am holding my breath. I let it out with a gasp when I hear my name.

By Emily C. Cornelius
First Place: Essays, Grades 9–12
College of William and Mary Writing Talent Search

Theme/Concept

C3

Identify the theme of this essay in one sentence.

Inference

C2

Did the author deserve to win the competition?
What evidence supports your answer?

Literary Elements

C1

The author of the essay experiences many emotions during the competition. Which emotions are experienced and how do you know?

THE COMPETITION

Creative Synthesis

D3

Write another version of the essay from the ninth player's point of view.

Summarizing

D2

In five sentences or less, summarize the author's competition experience.

Paraphrasing

D1

In your own words, describe the author's thoughts while the ninth musician is performing.

THE COMPETITION

Excerpts from *Common Sense*
by Thomas Paine

. . . I have heard it asserted by some, that as America hath flourished under her former connection with Great Britain, that the same connection is necessary towards her future happiness, and will always have the same effect. . . .We may as well assert, that because a child has thrived upon milk, that it is never to have meat; or that the first twenty years of our lives is to become a precedent for the next twenty. But even this is admitting more than is true, for I answer roundly, that America would have flourished as much, and probably much more, had no European power had any thing to do with her. The commerce by which she hath enriched herself are the necessaries of life, and will always have a market while eating is the custom of Europe. . . .

But Britain is the parent country, say some. Then the more shame upon her conduct. Even brutes do not devour their young; nor savages make war upon their families; wherefore the assertion, if true, turns to her reproach; but it happens not to be true, or only partly so . . . Europe, and not England, is the parent country of America. This new world hath been the asylum for the persecuted lovers of civil and religious liberty from every part of Europe. . . .

I challenge the warmest advocate for reconciliation to show a single advantage that this continent can reap, by being connected with Great Britain. I repeat the challenge, not a single advantage is derived. Our corn will fetch its price in any market in Europe, and our imported goods must be paid for, buy them where we will.

But the injuries and disadvantages we sustain by that connection are without number; and our duty to mankind at large, as well as to ourselves, instruct us to renounce the alliance: Because, any submission to, or dependence on Great Britain, tends directly to involve this continent in European wars and quarrels; and sets us at variance with nations, who would otherwise seek our friendship, and against whom, we have neither anger nor complaint. As Europe is our market for trade, we ought to form no partial connection with any part of it. . . .

As to government matters, it is not in the powers of Britain to do this continent justice: The business of it will soon be too weighty, and intricate, to be managed with any tolerable degree of convenience, by a power, so distant from us, and so very ignorant of us; for if they cannot conquer us, they cannot govern us. To be always running three or four thousand miles with a tale or a petition, waiting four or five months for an answer, which when obtained requires five or six more to explain it in, will in a few years be looked upon as folly and childishness—there was a time when it was proper, and there is a proper time for it to cease.

Small islands not capable of protecting themselves are the proper objects for kingdoms to take under their care; but there is something very absurd in supposing a continent to be perpetually governed by an island. In no instance hath nature made the satellite larger than its primary planet, and as England and America, with respect to each other, reverses the common order of nature, it is evident they belong to different systems: England to Europe—America to itself . . .

A government of our own is our natural right: And when a man seriously reflects on the precariousness of human affairs, he will become convinced, that it is infinitely wiser and safer, to form a constitution of our own in a cool deliberate manner, while we have it in our power, than to trust such an interesting event to time and chance. . . .

However strange it may appear to some, or however unwilling they may be to think so, matters not, but many strong and striking reasons may be given, to show, that nothing can settle our affairs as expeditiously as an open and determined declaration for independence. . . . Under our present denomination of British subjects we can neither be received nor heard abroad: The custom of all courts is against us, and will be so, until, by an independence, we take rank with other nations.

Generalizations

B3

What generalizations can you make about independence based on your list?

Classifications

B2

Classify your list into categories.

Details

B1

List the ways in which Paine thinks America should exert her independence.

EXCERPTS FROM COMMON SENSE

C3

Theme/Concept

What does Paine's essay say about the concept of freedom?

C2

Inference

What evidence does Paine give for not forming an alliance with Great Britain?

C1

Literary Elements

What kind of person is Thomas Paine? How do you know?

EXCERPTS FROM COMMON SENSE

Franklin D. Roosevelt's First Inaugural Address (Excerpt)

Saturday, March 4, 1933

I am certain that my fellow Americans expect that on my induction into the Presidency I will address them with a candor and a decision which the present situation of our Nation impels. This is preeminently the time to speak the truth, the whole truth, frankly and boldly. Nor need we shrink from honestly facing conditions in our country today. This great Nation will endure as it has endured, will revive and will prosper. So, first of all, let me assert my firm belief that the only thing we have to fear is fear itself—nameless, unreasoning, unjustified terror which paralyzes needed efforts to convert retreat into advance. In every dark hour of our national life a leadership of frankness and vigor has met with that understanding and support of the people themselves which is essential to victory. I am convinced that you will again give that support to leadership in these critical days.

In such a spirit on my part and on yours we face our common difficulties. They concern, thank God, only material things. Values have shrunken to fantastic levels; taxes have risen; our ability to pay has fallen; government of all kinds is faced by serious curtailment of income; the means of exchange are frozen in the currents of trade; the withered leaves of industrial enterprise lie on every side; farmers find no markets for their produce; the savings of many years in thousands of families are gone.

More important, a host of unemployed citizens face the grim problem of existence, and an equally great number toil with little return. Only a foolish optimist can deny the dark realities of the moment. . . .

Happiness lies not in the mere possession of money; it lies in the joy of achievement, in the thrill of creative effort. . . .

Recognition of the falsity of material wealth as the standard of success goes hand in hand with the abandonment of the false belief that public office and high political position are to be valued only by the standards of pride of place and personal profit; and there must be an end to a conduct in banking and in business which too often has given to a sacred trust the likeness of callous and selfish wrongdoing. Small wonder that confidence languishes, for it thrives only on honesty, on honor, on the sacredness of obligations, on faithful protection, on unselfish performance; without them it cannot live. Restoration calls, however, not for changes in ethics alone. This Nation asks for action, and action now. . . .

In the field of world policy I would dedicate this Nation to the policy of the good neighbor—the neighbor who resolutely respects himself and, because he does so, respects the rights of others—the neighbor who respects his obligations and respects the sanctity of his agreements in and with a world of neighbors. If I read the temper of our people correctly, we now realize as we have never realized before our interdependence on each other; that we can not merely take but we must give as well; that if we are to go forward, we must move as a trained and loyal army willing to sacrifice for the good of a common discipline, because without such discipline no progress is made, no leadership becomes effective. We are, I know, ready and willing to submit our lives and property to such discipline, because it makes possible a leadership which aims at a larger good. This I propose to offer, pledging that the larger purposes will bind upon us all a sacred obligation with a unity of duty hitherto evoked only in time of armed strife.

With this pledge taken, I assume unhesitatingly the leadership of this great army of our people dedicated to a disciplined attack upon our common problems.

We face the arduous days that lie before us in the warm courage of the national unity; with the clear consciousness of seeking old and precious moral values; with the clean satisfaction that comes from the stern performance of duty by old and young alike. We aim at the assurance of a rounded and permanent national life.

We do not destruct the future of essential democracy. The people of the United States have not failed. In their need they have registered a mandate that they want direct, vigorous action. They have asked for discipline and direction under leadership. They have made me the present instrument of their wishes. In the spirit of the gift I take it.

FRANKLIN D. ROOSEVELT'S FIRST INAUGURAL ADDRESS

Generalizations

B3

What generalizations can you make about life in the 1930s, based on your reading?

Classifications

B2

Classify your list into categories.

Details

B1

List the specific actions Franklin D. Roosevelt says are necessary to improve the lives of Americans in 1933.

Creative Synthesis

D3

Pretend you are one of the individuals who heard Roosevelt's speech. Write an essay or a letter to Roosevelt in response to his words.

Summarizing

D2

In five sentences or less, summarize what Franklin D. Roosevelt told the American people in his inaugural address.

Paraphrasing

D1

In your own words, paraphrase the following quotation: "Happiness lies not in the mere possession of money; it lies in the joy of achievement, in the thrill of creative effort."

FRANKLIN D. ROOSEVELT'S FIRST INAUGURAL ADDRESS

The Gettysburg Address
By Abraham Lincoln

Four score and seven years ago our fathers brought forth on this continent, a new nation, conceived in Liberty, and dedicated to the proposition that all men are created equal.

Now we are engaged in a great civil war, testing whether that nation, or any nation so conceived and so dedicated, can long endure. We are met on a great battlefield of that war. We have come to dedicate a portion of that field, as a final resting place for those who here gave their lives that that nation might live. It is altogether fitting and proper that we should do this.

But, in a larger sense, we can not dedicate—we can not consecrate—we can not hallow—this ground. The brave men, living and dead, who struggled here, have consecrated it, far above our poor power to add or detract. The world will little note, nor long remember what we say here, but it can never forget what they did here. It is for us the living, rather, to be dedicated here to the unfinished work which they who fought here have thus far so nobly advanced. It is rather for us to be here dedicated to the great task remaining before us—that from these honored dead we take increased devotion to that cause for which they gave the last full measure of devotion—that we here highly resolve that these dead shall not have died in vain—that this nation, under God, shall have a new birth of freedom—and that government of the people, by the people, for the people, shall not perish from the earth.

Theme/Concept

C3

What does Lincoln's address say about the concept of liberty?

Inference

C2

What inferences can you make about Lincoln's hopes for the future of the United States? What evidence supports your answer?

Literary Elements

C1

How does Lincoln characterize the soldiers who died during the Battle of Gettysburg? Support your answer.

THE GETTYSBURG ADDRESS

D3

Creative Synthesis

Pretend you are an interested party from the audience (e.g., mother, father, sibling of a soldier; a soldier; a congressional leader; the secretary of war) who has just heard the Gettysburg Address. How would you react to the message of Lincoln's speech? Create a reaction to the Gettysburg Address.

D2

Summarizing

In three sentences or less, summarize the message Lincoln is trying to convey to the American people.

D1

Paraphrasing

In your own words, paraphrase Lincoln's statement, "It is for us the living, rather, to be dedicated here to the unfinished work which they who fought here have thus far so nobly advanced."

THE GETTYSBURG ADDRESS

Legacy

On October 29, 1996, my Uncle Charlie died at the age of 90. He was actually my great-uncle, my grandmother's older brother, but everyone in our family, and most of the people in the small southern town where he lived, called him Uncle Charlie.

Uncle Charlie was one of my favorite people. He was 6' 4" tall and had a big, booming voice. He always wore freshly-ironed overalls and starched khaki shirts. But the thing that fascinated me most was that he was a near-genius in mathematics. He could multiply three- and four-digit numbers in his head faster than I could do them on a calculator, and he was never wrong. He read and pondered everything he could get his hands on—from newspapers (he always read the sports page first), to encyclopedias, to the labels of soup cans. He loved education more than anyone I have ever known, probably because he never had a chance for very much.

Uncle Charlie and my grandmother came from a family of eight children; she was the youngest, he was the oldest and only boy. Their father was a tenant farmer, and they lived several miles from the nearest town. The tiny, one-room country school Uncle Charlie and his sisters attended began in late October, after the crops had been harvested, and closed in mid-March, when it was time to plant. Their school year ran less than 5 months.

That old school is still standing, and Uncle Charlie took me there once. It was much smaller than my classroom, with cracks between the boards wider than a finger. It didn't take a vivid imagination to see how cold it would have been in winter, even in the South. There was no running water, and a stovepipe hole in the roof indicated that the only heat was a wood-burning stove.

I was horrified, but I tried not to show it, because Uncle Charlie talked about the place as if it were Harvard. He glowed as he told me how he was always first in mental arithmetic, and how he once "turned down" all the other children in the school in a spelling bee. He told me about the taffy pulls that were held at school on fall nights, and about the commencement exercises in the spring, where he once recited the whole Declaration of Independence from memory. When we left, he took some twine from his pocket and carefully tied the rusted hinges of the door shut. I remember thinking, "Why bother? What is there in this old place that anything could possibly hurt?" But now I understand: He was protecting his memories.

On the way home that day, Uncle Charlie showed me where his family's farmhouse had stood and the way he walked to school. It was a good 3 miles, most of it uphill. But he didn't talk about how far it was or tell tales of walking through the snow. He spoke with joy of the excitement of a bright October morning when you could hear the clang of the school bell far in the distance, of the games he and his sisters played on the way home from school, of picking wild grapes and muscadines that were all the sweeter for having been touched by an early frost.

In the winter of 1918, his father died in the great flu epidemic. Uncle Charlie's mother, a widow at 34, had no way to support her children except to farm, and no one to help her except Uncle Charlie. He quit his beloved school and became the breadwinner for his family. He was 12 years old.

As much as I sometimes say I'd like to, the idea of actually quitting school so young was as alien to me as the idea of relocating to another planet. "Didn't you mind?" I asked him once.

"Of course I minded," he said, his eyes fixed on some place in the distance that I could not see. "But I would have minded a whole lot more to see your grandma and the other little girls go hungry. After awhile I realized that your brain doesn't have to die just because you can't go to school. We didn't have many books, but we had a Bible, and I read it over and over, for the beauty of the words, not just the religion. One of the neighbor ladies had been a schoolteacher, and she taught me the names of all the stars. When I was ploughing late, trying to get the crop in, I'd watch them come out and name them over, one by one."

My uncle became a good farmer, but during the depths of the Depression even a good farmer could not make a living for nine people on a tenant farm. After several years the family moved to town, where Uncle Charlie and his mother supported the family by working in a cotton mill.

After all his sisters had graduated from high school and my grandmother, the youngest, had gone off to college, Uncle Charlie got married. He and his wife had two children. He carried their report cards in his pocket and became the town's most enthusiastic PTA member. His son enlisted in the Air Force and served 25 years, earning two college degrees while in the service. His daughter graduated from nursing school and became a pediatric nurse.

Uncle Charlie worked hard at the mill and eventually became a supervisor. During the late 1950s he asked my grandmother, then the head of the personnel department, to find him some workers who wouldn't quit as soon as they were trained. She asked if he'd be willing to try some mentally retarded students from the high school. He was, and in a couple of weeks, sent back word, "I want more just like these two. I don't know anything about this 'retarded' business, but these kids love a weaving loom like other kids their age love a hot rod."

A year or so later, my grandmother approached him with another proposition: Would he be willing to become the first supervisor to employ Black workers? It was a dangerous time; the local schools were about to be integrated, and feeling was running high. But Uncle Charlie never faltered: "I don't care what color they are. If they want to work, send 'em on."

Uncle Charlie told me that decision got him two things: a rock through his living room window and some of the best workers he ever supervised. I asked him if the rock didn't scare him, and he said, "No, because I had been there myself and knew it needed to be done. When we couldn't make it on the farm any more, the mill gave us a chance to earn a decent living. Black folks needed to feed their kids and send 'em to school, and they deserved the same chance we had. This country would be so much better off if everybody would stop hollering and realize that the other fellow wants the same thing you do: to take care of his family and give them a better life." He thought politicians made things worse: "George Wallace, many times he ran, I never voted for him for anything. I know they say he's changed here lately, but back in those days he was talking nothing but hate. To get my vote, a politician had to show he was capable of leading something more than a mob. I never did vote for a hating politician."

Uncle Charlie retired from the mill after 45 years and had a few quiet years of retirement, enjoying his newspapers and his garden, before his wife developed Alzheimer's. Her doctors recommended that he put her in a nursing home, but in 50 years of marriage they had never spent a night apart, and he was afraid she wouldn't be happy. On his small fixed income, he managed to hire caretakers and kept her at home until she died.

After his wife's death, we were afraid that Uncle Charlie would give up, but that was not his style. He did have one emotional crisis at the age of 86 when his beloved tractor broke down, and he couldn't decide whether to buy a new one. But typically, he decided to have faith in the future, bought the new tractor and went on supplying friends, relatives, and sometimes, total strangers, with vegetables from his huge garden.

When I started to school, I began sending him copies of stories and poems I had written. He always replied, sending me small gifts of encouragement: stickers saying "Excellent!" and "Far Out!" purchased at the local Wal-Mart, a subscription to *National Geographic*, and on one memorable occasion, my first fountain pen ("because every serious writer ought to have one.")

He was so strong that we began to think of him as invincible, so we were shocked a year ago when his doctors told us that what we thought was bronchitis was metastatic cancer. When the doctors told Uncle Charlie, he was typically calm. "I always said I wanted to leave this world with my hair, my teeth, and all my marbles," he said, "and it looks like I'm going to make it."

I saw Uncle Charlie for the last time in September. I realized he was dying and didn't want to leave, but school was starting, and he would not hear of my staying longer. I knew I wouldn't be able to say good-bye. But Uncle Charlie was coming to the end of a long lifetime of honesty, and he didn't talk in circles as people in these situations often do. He took both my hands in his big, work-roughened ones, looked me straight in the eye and said the simplest and strongest of words, "Good-bye. Keep studying hard. I love you, and I'm proud of you."

He died on a bright, blue October morning when the last of the wild grapes and muscadines were hanging heavy on the vines. It was the kind of day when eight decades earlier a little barefoot boy had joyously run toward the sound of a distant bell.

This is a nation of honors. We have honor rolls for high schools and dean's lists for colleges. We give the Congressional Medal of Honor to our bravest soldiers. We award Pulitzer Prizes, Oscars, and Heisman Trophies. Every newspaper publishes lists of Nobel Prize winners. Shouldn't we also have an honor roll for people who never had a chance to win academic honors, but for a lifetime were good citizens, parents, workers, friends? If we ever have the compassion and good sense to make this happen, I have a nomination for the first name on the list: Charles Fletcher Stevenson.

I learned many things from Uncle Charlie. Always read the sports page first. Value your education; not everyone has the chance. Don't vote for hatin' politicians. And most of all: Love of family, country, our fellow men—is the foundation of everything worthwhile that we do in this sweet life. Love is the beginning. There is no end.

By Elisabeth Gorey
First Place: Essays, Grades 4–6
The College of William and Mary
Writing Talent Search

Generalizations

B3

What generalizations can you make about the concept of family from your list? About love?

Classifications

B2

Classify your list into categories.

Details

B1

List all of the things the author admires about her Uncle Charlie.

LEGACY

Creative Synthesis

D3

How would Uncle Charlie react if he read this essay? Write an essay or a letter in response from Uncle Charlie's point of view.

Summarizing

D2

In five sentences or less, summarize the author's memories of Uncle Charlie.

Paraphrasing

D1

In your own words, describe Uncle Charlie's school experience.

LEGACY

Moving Pictures Evoke Concern, 1922

*(Speech by Senator Henry Myers,
from the* Congressional Record, *June 29, 1922)*

The motion picture is a great invention, and it has become a powerful factor for good or bad in our civilization. It has great educational power for good or bad. It may educate young people in the ways of good citizenship or in ways of dissoluteness, extravagance, wickedness, and crime. It furnishes recreation, diversion, and amusement at a cheap price to many millions of our people—largely the young. It is the only form of amusement that most people can afford.

Through motion pictures the young and the old may be taught that honesty is the best policy; that virtue and worth are rewarded; that industry leads to success. Those who live in the country or in small interior towns, and who never visit large cities, may see pictured the skyscrapers, the crowded streets, the rush and jam of metropolitan cities. Those who live in the interior, and never see the seacoast, may see on the screen the great docks and wharves of seaports. Those who live in crowded cities, and never see the country or get a glimpse of country life, may have depicted to them all the beauties of rural life and scenery. All may see scenes of the luxuriant Tropics, the grandeur of Alpine Mountains, polar conditions, life in the Orient. The cities, palaces, cathedrals, ports, rural life, daily routine, scenic attractions, mode of living of every country on the globe, may be brought to our eyes. The industry may be made an education to the young.

However, from all accounts, the movie business has been conducted with low standards. Those who own and control the industry seem to think that the sensual, the sordid, the phases of fast life, the ways of extravagance, the risqué, the paths of shady life, draw the greatest crowds and so they are out to get money, no matter what the effect upon the public, young or old.

I have no doubt young criminals got their ideas of the romance of crime from moving pictures. I believe moving pictures are doing as much harm today as saloons did in the days of the open saloon—especially to the young. They are running day and night, Sunday and every day, the year round and in most places without any regulation by censorship. I would not abolish movies. They can be made a great force for good. I would close them on Sunday and regulate them week days by judicious censorship.

When we look to the source of the moving pictures, the material for them, the people who pose for them, we need not wonder that many of the pictures are destructive. . . .

These are some of the characters from whom the young people of today are deriving a large part of their education, views of life, and character-forming habits. From these sources our young people gain much of their views of life, inspiration, and education. Rather a poor source, is it not?

Consequences and Implications

A3

What does Myers believe are the implications of allowing the motion picture industry to continue uncensored? If movies were censored, what would be the consequences?

Cause and Effect

A2

Does Myers believe motion pictures cause crime? Support your answer.

Sequencing

A1

List, for each paragraph, the main ideas Myers makes in his speech.

MOVING PICTURES EVOKE CONCERN, 1922

Creative Synthesis

D3

Write a one-page speech about how movies affect young people today.

Summarizing

D2

What is the overall main idea of Senator Myers' speech?

Paraphrasing

D1

In your own words, paraphrase the following quotation: "Through motion pictures the young and the old may be taught that honesty is the best policy; that virtue and worth are rewarded; that industry leads to success."

MOVING PICTURES EVOKE CONCERN, 1922

Washington's Letter to His Wife Martha

June 18, 1775

My Dearest:

    I am now set down to write you on a subject which fills me with inexpressible concern, and this concern is greatly aggravated and increased, when I reflect upon the uneasiness I know it will cause you. It has been determined in Congress, that the whole army raised for the defense of the American cause shall be put under my care, and that it is necessary for me to proceed immediately to Boston to take command of it.

    You may believe me, my dear Patsy, when I assure you, in the most solemn manner, that, so far from seeking this appointment, I have used every endeavor in my power to avoid it, not only from my unwillingness to part with you and the family, but from a consciousness of its being a trust too great for my capacity, and that I should enjoy more real happiness in one month with you at home than I have the most distant prospect of finding abroad, if my stay were to be seven times seven years. But as it has been a kind of destiny that has thrown me upon this service, I shall hope that my undertaking it is designed to answer some good purpose. . . .

    It was utterly out of my power to refuse the appointment, without exposing my character to such censures, as would have reflected dishonor upon myself, and given pain to my friends. This, I am sure, could not, and ought not, to be pleasing to you, and must have lessened me considerably in my own esteem. I shall rely, therefore, confidently on that Providence which has heretofore preserved and been bountiful to me, not doubting but that I shall return safe to you in the fall. I shall feel no pain from the toil of the danger of the campaign; my unhappiness will flow from the uneasiness I know you will feel from being left alone. I therefore beg, that you will summon your whole fortitude, and pass your time as agreeably as possible. Nothing will give me so much sincere satisfaction as to hear this, and to hear it from your own pen. . . .

WASHINGTON'S LETTER TO HIS WIFE MARTHA

Consequences and Implications

A3

What might have happened if Washington had refused to lead the army?

Cause and Effect

A2

What effect might Washington's absence have on his wife Martha?

Sequencing

A1

What major events does Washington discuss in paragraph 1, paragraph 2, and paragraph 3? Why do you think he chose this order?

Theme/Concept

C3

How does Washington's letter address the concept of honor?

Inference

C2

Does George Washington want to lead the American army? What evidence supports your position?

Literary Elements

C1

What kind of person is George Washington? Support your answer with evidence from the text.

WASHINGTON'S LETTER TO HIS WIFE MARTHA

Why Own a House When You Can Own an R.V.?

Today's life is so hectic nobody spends any time in their homes with their families. Leisurely evenings at home have given way to hectic evenings on the road. People are always on the go, so why not take the house with you? That's where the recreational vehicle (R.V.) comes in. When you have to run errands, or take your kids to soccer or basketball practice, your time could also be spent cleaning your house, doing your laundry or making a meal.

We've created a world where the goal is to make things faster and to allow us to do two or three things at once. Traditional mail has been replaced by overnight mail, e-mail, and faxes, and home cooked meals have been replaced by fast food or microwave meals. We have so many things to make our lives "easier," but we never have time to use any of them.

One solution for anyone who says "I spend no time in my house," is to trade your expensive mortgage for a house you can take with you. After all, with a good hook-up, an R.V. contains all the necessities of life: a bathroom, running water, kitchens, beds, satellite TV, cellular phones, electric lights, and, of course, a moving vehicle. In the near future, our communities will simply be R.V. lots so families can drive from their home lot to temporary lots that provide home-like settings for busy families on the go.

Another solution would be to cut back your busy schedules and stay home more often. Do one thing at a time and live for today. Sit back once in a while, relax, and take the time to enjoy your life.

By Robert J. Hidy
Second Place: Essays, Grades 4–5
The College of William and Mary Writing Talent Search

Generalizations

B3

What generalizations can you make about
how families spend time today?

Classifications

B2

Classify your list into categories.

Details

B1

Make a list of at least 25 things that keep families busy.

WHY OWN A HOUSE WHEN YOU CAN OWN AN R.V.?

WHY OWN A HOUSE WHEN YOU CAN OWN AN R.V.?

Theme/Concept

C3

What ideas are expressed in the essay about the concept of time?

Inference

C2

Do you agree or disagree with the author about trading in your house for an R.V.? What evidence supports your answer?

Literary Elements

C1

Write a paragraph or draw a picture of the type of family being characterized in this essay.

CHAPTER

2

Poetry

Chapter 2 includes the selected readings and accompanying question sets for each poetry selection. Each reading is followed by one or two sets of questions; each set is aligned to one of the four ladder skills. For *Jacob's Ladder 3,* the skills covered by each selection are as follows:

A Corn-Song

By Paul Laurence Dunbar

On the wide veranda white,
In the purple failing light,
Sits the master while the sun is lowly burning;
And his dreamy thoughts are drowned
In the softly flowing sound
Of the corn-songs of the field-hands slow returning.

Oh, we hoe de co'n
Since de ehly mo'n;
Now de sinkin' sun
Says de day is done.

O'er the fields with heavy tread,
Light of heart and high of head,
Though the halting steps be labored, slow, and weary;
Still the spirits brave and strong
Find a comforter in song,
And their corn-song rises ever loud and cheery.

Oh, we hoe de co'n
Since de ehly mo'n;
Now de sinkin' sun
Says de day is done.

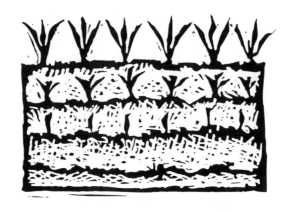

A3

Consequences and Implications

The "end of the day" and the "setting sun" have different effects on the master and on the field hands. The first stanza describes the effect on the master. The second stanza, after the first refrain, describes the effect on the field hands. What does the poet imply about the meaning of the end of the day for each one?

A2

Cause and Effect

Find examples of cause and effect in the poem. What causes the field hands to sing? What is the effect of the song on the master? What is the effect of the song on the field hands? What causes the field hands to return slowly? Make a list of as many examples as you can find.

A1

Sequencing

Describe the sequence of events in the poem from the point of view of the master. What is he doing? Look carefully at each line. Then describe the sequence of events in the poem from the point of view of the field hands. What are they doing? The actions should show a sequence.

A CORN-SONG

Name: _____ Date: _____

Creative Synthesis

D3

Using this poem as a model, write a new poem about a teacher and his or her students at the end of the day. Stanza 1 should describe the teacher at the end of the day. Write a 4 line refrain similar to Stanzas 2 and 4 that are sung by students. Stanza 3 should describe the students at the end of the day.

Summarizing

D2

In your own words, tell what is happening in the poem.

Paraphrasing

D1

Rewrite Stanza 1 in your own words. Use a dictionary to look up any unfamiliar words.

A CORN-SONG

The Harp

In the realm of Ireland,
The moon began to shine,
But the fever swept the little town
And blinded Caroline.

All the beautiful things to see,
And all she sees is night,
All is black and icy darkness,
In that world without light.

So she learned to play the harp,
And it grew to become her life,
Even though she learned other instruments,
Like the fiddle and the fife.

Nothing matched the silver harp,
Its strings so smooth and cold,
For it seemed to give her hope,
In her life that seemed so old.

For grand kings and queens desired
To hear her songs,
So pure they touched the heart,
The silver strings would become as one,
To sound like a morning lark.

Yet the fever never ended,
And she continued to decay,
But her guide never left her side,
Till she spoke to him one day.

"I remember the days I could see,
A tree's bark seems like gold.
So be thankful that you can see,
Your own hand when you're twelve years old."

Then he replied to her so quick,
"They say when you die all shall be night,
But for you, you are blind,
So for you, shall it be light?"

By Nathan D. Little
Third Place: Poetry, Grades 6–8
Reflections, 1997–1998, Talent Search for Promising Student Writers

Generalizations

B3

Make at least three generalizations about disabilities from Exercise B2.

Classifications

B2

How can you organize your list of disabilities? Create as many categories as you need. Label each list with a title that explains the list.

Details

B1

Caroline has a disability—she is blind. Make a list of as many disabilities as you can think of in 5 minutes.

THE HARP

Theme/Concept

C3

What "Big Idea" do you think the author wants us to learn from the poem? Why did the author tell this story? Write a paragraph supporting your opinion.

Inference

C2

Make a list of Caroline's characteristics. Next to each trait, write a word or phrase from the poem that supports your choice of characteristics.

Literary Elements

C1

Use a graphic organizer to describe Caroline. What does she look like? How old is she? What does she like to do? What positive qualities does she have? What kind of attitude does she have?

THE HARP

I Am The Moon

When the sun's light has gone away,
I show my single, pale, lifeless eye.
My star strewn cloak adorns my dark shoulders,
and covers my once blue body.
Long ago, my eye was bright,
but now it is drowned out by our city lights and smoke.
Still I persevere!
Finally, the sun peeks her golden face over the horizon,
and I go to pull my cloak to the other side of the world.

By Laura P. Fletcher
Third Place, Poetry, Grades 4–5
Reflections 1998–1999 Talent Search for Promising Student Writers

Generalizations

B3

Using your lists, create at least three generalizations you can make about the moon. Use evidence from the poem.

Classifications

B2

Group these characteristics into classifications. Give each group a title.

Details

B1

Make a list of characteristics of the moon according to the poem.

I AM THE MOON

Theme/Concept

C3

Using this poem for a model, write a poem of your own that uses imagery.

Inference

C2

How would you describe the moon in this poem?

Literary Elements

C1

This poet uses imagery. Imagery is the use of words or phrases that appeal to any sense or any combination of senses. Make a T-Chart. On the left, list examples of imagery. On the right, list the sense or senses that the imagery stimulates.

Imagery examples	Senses stimulated

I AM THE MOON

If

By Rudyard Kipling

If you can keep your head when all about you
Are losing theirs and blaming it on you;
If you can trust yourself when all men doubt you,
But make allowance for their doubting too;
If you can wait and not be tired by waiting,
Or, being lied about, don't deal in lies,
Or, being hated, don't give way to hating,
And yet don't look too good, nor talk too wise;
If you can dream—and not make dreams your master;
If you can think—and not make thoughts your aim;
If you can meet with triumph and disaster
And treat those two imposters just the same;
If you can bear to hear the truth you've spoken
Twisted by knaves to make a trap for fools,
Or watch the things you gave your life to, broken,
And stoop and build 'em up with wornout tools;
If you can make one heap of all your winnings
And risk it on one turn of pitch-and-toss,
And lose, and start again at your beginnings
And never breath a word about your loss;
If you can force your heart and nerve and sinew
To serve your turn long after they are gone,
And so hold on when there is nothing in you
Except the Will which says to them: "Hold on";
If you can talk with crowds and keep your virtue,
Or walk with kings—nor lose the common touch;
If neither foes nor loving friends can hurt you;
If all men count with you, but none too much;
If you can fill the unforgiving minute
With sixty seconds' worth of distance run—
Yours is the Earth and everything that's in it,
And—which is more—you'll be a Man my son!

Kipling wrote "If" with Dr. Leander Starr Jameson in mind. In 1895, Jameson led about 500 of his countrymen in a failed raid against the Boers, in southern Africa. What became known as the Jameson Raid was later cited as a major factor in bringing about the Boer War of 1899 to 1902. But, the story as recounted in Britain was quite different. The British defeat was interpreted as a victory and Jameson portrayed as a daring hero.

Theme/Concept

C3

The theme of a poem is the "Big Idea" the author wants to get across. What Big Idea do you think this author wanted to communicate? How did you choose this theme?

Inference

C2

For each descriptive statement from Exercise C1, write a statement from the poem that proves your idea.

Literary Elements

C1

This poem was written to a military leader. From the author's statements, how would you describe this military leader?

IF

Creative Synthesis

D3

Choose an occupation: _____ (job title). Using the summary statements from Exercise D2 as an example, write two statements that give important characteristics of someone in your chosen occupation. Write a new, eight-line poem that ends with the line: And which is more, you will be a _____, my son/daughter. Fill in the blank with the occupation of your choice.

Summarizing

D2

IF

Using Exercise D1, write one or two sentences that summarize the stanza.

Paraphrasing

D1

Reread the poem "If" by Rudyard Kipling. Choose the stanza that you think is the easiest to understand. Rewrite the ideas from the stanza using your own words.

The Lament of the Frog Prince

Within this blazing hall
the light of a thousand
candles rivals the harsh,
glittering fire of diamonds.
The screech of violins
sears my brain. Voices trill
with mirthless laughter.
My eager subjects wait.
Their false, cunning smiles
could grace the jaws of jackals.
My lady bows before me,
and by the sound of rustling silk,
her perfume like a memory
of a thousand night flowers.
I am transported
to a time and place of
cool darkness, the whisper
of a breeze caressing rushes
at water's edge, the scent
of creamy clusters of blossoms
swaying gently in the wind,
the soft lap of waves against
the shore. I long to
bury myself in the
comforting ooze of mud.

Ah! If I had only known
I was trading my whole
world for the pleasure
of a single kiss!

By Elisabeth B. Gorey
Honorable Mention: Poetry, Grades 6–8
Reflections 1997–1998, Talent Search for Promising Student Writers

THE LAMENT OF THE FROG PRINCE

Consequences and Implications

A3

What are the long-term and short-term consequences of the frog's kiss? What does the story imply about the Prince's feelings about his life? Explain your answer, using phrases from the poem to support your ideas.

Cause and Effect

A2

Cause and effect can be represented using a fishbone graphic organizer. Using the kiss as the cause, fill in the effects on each of the diagonal "bones."

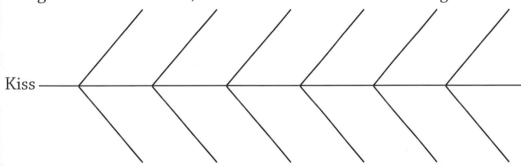

Kiss

Sequencing

A1

Sometimes stories are told in chronological (time) order. This poem is told from the perspective of looking back over a lifetime. Create a timeline of the Frog Prince's life based on the poem.

Theme/Concept

C3

This poem is based on a fairy tale but written from a different character's point of view. Choose a fairy tale such as "Goldilocks and the Three Bears," "Hansel and Gretel," or "Jack and the Beanstalk." Write a poem from a point of view that is different from the original story.

Inference

C2

What can you infer about the prince? Use evidence from the poem to support your inference.

Literary Elements

C1

The author uses metaphor to describe things that are really different. Give examples of metaphor from the poem. Explain what each metaphor means.

THE LAMENT OF THE FROG PRINCE

The Road Not Taken
By Robert Frost

Two roads diverged in a yellow wood,
And sorry I could not travel both
And be one traveler, long I stood
And looked down one as far as I could
To where it bent in the undergrowth.

Then took the other, as just as fair,
And having perhaps the better claim,
Because it was grassy and wanted wear;
Though as for that the passing there
Had worn them really about the same.

And both that morning equally lay
In leaves no step had trodden black.
Oh, I kept the first for another day!
Yet knowing how way leads on to way,
I doubted if I should ever come back.

I shall be telling this with a sigh
Somewhere ages and ages hence:
Two roads diverged in a wood, and I—
I took the one less traveled by,
And that has made all the difference.

Consequences and Implications

A3

The last stanza describes the consequences of the act of choosing one path rather than the other. What does the author imply about his choice?

Cause and Effect

A2

Find at least three examples of cause and effect in the poem. List them.

Sequencing

A1

Make a timeline showing what the character did in the poem.

THE ROAD NOT TAKEN

Theme/Concept

C3

What do you think is the theme of the poem? (Remember that the theme is the "Big Idea" the author wants the reader to understand.)

Inference

C2

Use words and phrases from the poem to support or prove your description from Activity C1.

Literary Elements

C1

Describe the character from the poem.

THE ROAD NOT TAKEN

Sinking Sunset

I bob up and down,
Up and down, up and down.
The orange gold rays
Of the sunset
Fall on the shimmering water.
My boat rises and falls.
Rises and falls, rises and falls.
I bob up and down.
Up and down, up and down.
Splash! Splash! Splash!
A rotten timber hits
The shimmering water
Disturbing it, shaking it.
Splash! Splash! Splash!
Wood falls and falls.
The boat slowly sinks.
I, screaming, screaming.
The boat, sinking, sinking.
My mind goes black.
Then nothingness, nothingness.
A single piece of wet, rotten timber
Bobs up and down.
Up and down, up and down.

By Sarah Vogelsong
Second Place: Poetry, Grades 4–6
Reflections 1996–1997 Talent Search for Promising Student Writers

Consequences and Implications

A3

Choose one consequence listed in Activity A2. Create a fishbone organizer with this consequence listed as a cause. Name as many new possible consequences as you can.

Cause and Effect

A2

Sometimes events have more than one cause and more than one effect. What are the causes of the sinking boat? What are the effects of the sinking boat?

Sequencing

A1

Make a timeline showing the events from the poem.

SINKING SUNSET

Theme/Concept

C3

The title is "Sinking Sunset." How is this title related to the events of the poem? Write one or more paragraphs to compare the title of the poem to the story in the poem. How are they connected?

Inference

C2

What happens to the character in the poem? How do you know? Write one well-developed paragraph explaining your idea. Use evidence from the poem to support your idea.

Literary Elements

C1

Find at least five examples of repetition (the repeating of words, phrases, or lines).

Find at least five examples of onomatopoeia (the use of words that imitate sounds.)

SINKING SUNSET

Sunset

By Mary Weston Fordham

All hail! thou gorgeous sunset,
With thy gold and purple clouds,
Tinting the vast horizon,
Like shadowy, fleecy shrouds.

The mountain crests are glowing,
The hills are crimson dyed,
The very air seems blushing,
Bathed in thy amber tide.

Soon the twilight shadows falling
Will thy glory chase away,
And weary man will welcome
The closing of the day.

Then the moon in silvery brightness,
Will show her pale, sad face;
And the stars as her attendants,
Will stud infinite space.

Low down amid the valley
Soon we'll hear the night-bird's song,
Calling softly to the south wind,
That the day of toil is done.

Then hail! thou glorious sunset,
Who in fullness can portray
The varied, wondrous beauty
Of a summer's sunset day.

Generalizations

B3

Write two generalizations about sunset.

Classifications

B2

Divide the events listed in Activity B1 into groups.
Create a title for each group.

Details

B1

Make a list of events that happen at sunset.

SUNSET

Theme/Concept

C3

Dawn is the time when the sun is just rising. Using the model of "Sunset," write a poem about dawn.

Inference

C2

What can you infer about the author's opinion of sunset from the tone of the poem? Give examples from the poem as evidence.

Literary Elements

C1

Metaphor, simile, and personification are three poetic devices. Find examples of each in the poem.

SUNSET

The Visit

By Elizabeth Outlaw

As sure as the sunrise, the old man wakes.

This day is like every other Saturday:

Climbing out of bed, he draws up his overalls,
Never failing to put on his best Sunday shirt.
The old man then carefully lathers his face,
shaves with slow, deliberate strokes,
and gingerly pats the remaining white specks with a warm facecloth.

The old man gathers up his coins like every other Saturday
and puts them in a brown paper sack.
He takes note of the time on the old kitchen clock:
Half past seven.

Brown paper sack clinched in one hand, the keys to his truck in the other,
The old man begins his journey like every other Saturday.

Winding through the dusty Georgia roads
On the way to the "Big City,"
this is the country that the old man knows so well.
"Like the back of my hand," he would say.
The old man and his truck become one with the landscape.

Nearing signs of civilization,
the old man automatically sits up straighter in the cab.
He glances in his rearview mirror before making the turn
at the first red light like he does every other Saturday.

The old man parks in the visitor lot and turns off the ignition.
He slowly reaches for the brown paper sack and pauses—
'though he has made this trip so many times before, it is never easy.
Walking through the gate of chained links and barbed wire,
the old man approaches the window.

"I'm here to see Wade Davidson," he says in a soft, feeble voice
to the woman behind the paned glass.
"Wade Davidson, my grandson."

A3

Consequences and Implications

Where do you think the grandson is? What evidence can you find in the poem to support your conclusion? What do you think the old man will do with the bag of coins? What evidence from the poem supports your idea?

A2

Cause and Effect

Find at least three examples of cause and effect in the poem. Use a graphic organizer to illustrate the cause and effect relationships you found.

A1

Sequencing

Make a timeline of activities the old man does every other Saturday.

THE VISIT

Generalizations

B3

Make at least two generalizations about the old man in the poem.
Use details from the poem to support your generalizations.

Classifications

B2

Group the characteristics from Activity B1
and create a title for each group.

Details

B1

Make a list of the old man's characteristics.
Use details from the poem to create your list.

THE VISIT

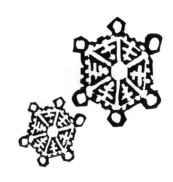

A Winter Morning

The morning is silent,
Through the fogged windows you can see the snowflakes falling,
Returning to the earth from their summer home in the heavens,
They land on silver barrettes with a whispered clink.

The frost covered grass is like a gloved hand, of a young lady,
Thin, and protected from the wind.

All the plump pumpkins are replaced by towering evergreens,
Waiting to be cut down and dressed royally,
Displayed as a piece of art.

People snuggle under downy comforters,
Not daring to leave the warmth of their beds for the chill of the room.

Sleek, golden handbells are performers for all,
Singing and dancing with their human partners,
They bring joy and spirit to the cold ears of everyone.

Experience promises us this time every year,
Faith makes us believe it will always return.

As red fires crackle and bare trees sleep,
Winter has returned.

By Kathryn E. Tickner
Honorable Mention: Poetry, Grades 6–8
Reflections: An Anthology of Award-Winning Works
1998–1999 Talent Search for Promising Student Authors

Consequences and Implications

A3

A generalization is a general statement that applies to a group of things. Make at least one generalization about each of your groups from Activity A2.

Cause and Effect

A2

Create lists from Activity A1. Group the details by their characteristics and create a title for each group.

Sequencing

A1

Make a list of examples from the poem that let the reader know it is winter time.

A WINTER MORNING

Generalizations

B3

What generalizations or broad statements can you make about art across cultures and time periods? Try to identify at least two, based on your work with Ladders B1 & B2.

Classifications

B2

How would you classify these features?

Details

B1

What are the features of the arts described in the text?
List as many as you can find.

A WINTER MORNING

CHAPTER

3

Nonfiction

Chapter 3 includes the selected readings and accompanying question sets for each nonfiction selection. Each reading is followed by one or two sets of questions; each set is aligned to one of the four ladder skills.

For *Jacob's Ladder 3*, the skills covered by each selection are as follows:

Economics 101

Have you ever heard adults talking about the economy? Have you wondered what they were talking about? Well, an economy is a collection of activities related to how a country manages its money and resources. It also is a way for a country to provide its citizens with what they want and need. Some of the most important components of American economy are trade, goods and services, producers, consumers, supply and demand, and free enterprise.

Trade

Trade first began with bartering. The word *barter* means "to trade." A long time ago, humans fulfilled their basic needs by hunting, gathering, building their own shelter, and carrying water from natural sources. As humans began to gain more knowledge, they wanted to make the fulfillment of basic needs easier. For example, they wanted to find ways to divert water to their homes and crops so they did not have to carry it in buckets. They also wanted to find ways to make feeding and sheltering their families less time consuming. People began to limit the kind of work they would do. For example, one man would decide that he really enjoyed hunting so he would be a hunter whereas another man would decide he really liked building things so he would become a carpenter. Then, when the hunter needed a house built, he would give the carpenter some of the meat he had hunted. In return, the carpenter would build him a house. These kinds of trades were the beginning of the barter system.

Soon, people wanted to make trade easier as well. Let's assume the hunter paid the carpenter in two deer. The carpenter then must find a way to get the two deer home; he had to carry them around with him. He may not have had the time, energy, or resources to move two deer. To make trade easier, people began using beads, shells, small animals, and crops such as corn as forms of money. A certain number of beads would be worth a certain amount of money. The carpenter could then take the beads he had earned to the hunter. The hunter would give him a certain amount of meat for a certain amount of beads. This way, the carpenter did not need to carry around meat until he needed it and was prepared to do so.

Money then evolved from beads, shells, animals, and crops to different sized lumps of various metals such as silver, copper, and gold. The lumps of metal worked well, but it was difficult to determine how much metal should be traded for certain things. For example, a woman might want to buy 42 pounds of corn from a farmer. She might have one big gold lump and one small copper lump. If she gave the farmer the big gold lump, then she would be paying him too much. But, if she gave him the small copper lump then she would not be paying enough. To solve this problem, people began pressing the metal into crude coins that were a little larger than today's half dollar. The coins had a predetermined value, making fair trade easier. As trade became more common, people noticed that the coins were really heavy in their pockets. They wanted an easier way to carry their money. Paper money was first made in 1690. It was the precursor to the paper money we use today.

Today, we still use money to buy things. When we buy school clothes, we are trading with the textile industry; we give them money, they give us clothes. When we go to a restaurant, we are trading money for food. And, each time your parents are paid at work, they are trading their expertise and knowledge of their job for money.

Goods and Services

Goods and services are the things that are traded within our economy. Goods are the different kinds of merchandise you can touch and feel. Look around the room; how many goods do you see? The chair you are sitting in is a good because you can touch it and someone paid money to buy it. The book you are reading also is a good for the same reasons. Services are when you pay someone to do some kind of work for you. For example, when the sink backs up your mom or dad may call the plumber. The plumber comes to your house and fixes the sink. Your parents have paid someone to do a certain kind of work for them. The plumber has provided them with a service.

Think about a restaurant. Is the restaurant itself a good or a service? What about the food? What about the work that the waiters, waitresses, and cooks do?

Producers and Consumers

In order for trade to function properly, there must be producers and consumers. We have all been both at various times in our lives. Producers are people and companies who make or grow goods to sell or provide a service that people can buy. For example, the farmer who grows strawberries is a producer of strawberries that he will sell to grocery stores. A person who provides tutoring for students after school is a producer of a service, or something he or she does for other people. Producers are always trying to make a profit, which means they are trying to get more money than they spend. The strawberry farmer hopes to sell his strawberries for a higher price than it cost him to grow the berries. The tutor is hoping to make more money than he or she spends on books, tutoring space, transportation, pencils, and other needs.

A consumer is a person who buys the goods and services that are for sale. If you buy strawberries from the grocery store, then you are the consumer. If you pay someone to tutor you in math, then you are the consumer.

Supply and Demand

Supply and demand keep the economy running smoothly. Supply refers to the amount of a particular good or service that is available to consumers. Demand refers to how much of a good or service the consumers are demanding from the producers. Maintaining balance between supply and demand is very important. Here is an example: have you ever seen a commercial for a new toy or game that you really wanted? You decide that you want to spend your allowance money to buy it. But, when you go to the store, you find they are all sold out of the item you want. After visiting several other stores, you learn they are sold out, also! Now you are really frustrated. This is an example of too little supply to meet the consumer demand. On the other hand, it would not be good for business if the producer made too many of a particular toy or game. Have you ever been in a store and seen shelves full of certain items that no one seems to want? This is an example of not enough demand for the supply produced.

Producers must pay close attention to consumers in order to get the balance between supply and demand just right. They need to listen to consumers' demands and make sure they produce enough of the goods and services that are most wanted. They also need to make sure they do not produce too many goods and services that are wanted by only a few consumers.

Free Enterprise

Free enterprise is a fancy way to say "competition." Free enterprise keeps the American economy moving. Producers are constantly competing with each other for consumers. Imagine there are two ice cream trucks in your neighborhood. One ice cream truck sells ice cream sandwiches for $1.50. The second ice cream truck decides to sell ice cream sandwiches for $1.00. Who will you buy your ice cream sandwich from? Probably the second truck! In order to keep customers and stay in the free enterprise competition, the first truck might lower the price of ice cream sandwiches to 75 cents. However, producers must be careful. The ice cream truck owners do not want to lower the price of their ice cream sandwiches below what it costs to buy them. They want to provide the consumer with the lowest, most competitive price while still earning a profit.

Supply and demand also contribute to free enterprise. When the demand for a good or service increases, then people are willing to pay more money for it. Therefore, high demand raises the price of goods and services. However, when the demand for a good or service decreases, then the price people are willing to pay also decreases. Low demand lowers the price of goods and services. Producers must pay careful attention to the demand of goods and services and adjust their prices accordingly.

Sometimes, producers want to buy the companies of all of the other producers who provide the same good or service they do. If there were no other companies making the same thing, then they could charge as much money as they wanted and consumers would have no choice but to pay it. When one company buys all the other companies making the same product, it is called a *monopoly*. In the United States, monopolies are against the law. Why do you think this is so?

Do you feel like you have a better understanding of economy now? The next time you hear grown ups talking about it, let them know what you have learned.

Consequences and Implications

A3

What are the implications of an economy based on the idea of supply and demand and free enterprise?

Cause and Effect

A2

Imagine that monopolies were not illegal in the United States. What effect would this change have on the economy? Why?

Sequencing

A1

List the events of the history of trade in order.

ECONOMICS 101

Creative Synthesis

D3

Draw a picture that illustrates the American economy. Think about all the components discussed in the text before you begin drawing.

Summarizing

D2

If someone asked you to explain the American economy, what would you tell him or her? Write your response in no more than 5 sentences. Make sure you capture the main ideas.

Paraphrasing

D1

Re-read the section, "Trade." In your own words, paraphrase the evolution of money.

ECONOMICS 101

Mass, Volume, and Density

The three mathematical concepts of mass, volume, and density are all used to describe different characteristics of objects.

Mass

Mass is the amount of matter in a given object. It is the total number of subatomic particles—protons, electrons, and neutrons—that the object contains. The measurement of mass is expressed in grams. Although mass and weight appear very similar, they are not the same thing. Weight is the mass of an object multiplied by the pull of Earth's gravity on the object. Consider this scenario: As you may know, you weigh less on the moon than you do on Earth. However, your mass remains exactly the same whether you are on the moon or on the Earth. The difference in your weight is attributed to the strength of the Earth's gravitational pull. When you are on Earth, the gravitational pull is, not surprisingly, stronger. When you travel far from the Earth to the moon, the strength of the Earth's gravitational pull is weakened and, therefore, you weigh less. The moon's gravitational pull is so small that it does not make much difference.

Volume

Volume measures the space an object occupies and is expressed in cubic centimeters. Every object occupies a certain amount of space within the universe. The volume of regularly shaped objects, such as cubes, spheres, and cones can be determined by formulas. For example, to find the volume of a cube, you multiply the lengths of the three sides (height, depth, and width). Therefore, if a cube has a height of 2 centimeters, a width of 2 centimeters, and a depth of 2 centimeters, then its volume is 8 cubic centimeters.

The volume of irregularly shaped objects is more difficult to determine. The theory of water displacement often is used in these situations. Do you know how water displacement works? First, you put water into a container and mark the level of the water. Then, the object is placed in the water, which causes the water level to rise. The new water level is marked. The volume of the irregularly shaped object is determined by the difference between the original water level and the water level when the object was in the container of water.

Density

Density is the relationship between the mass of an object and the object's volume. In other words, density describes how much stuff is in how much space or how compact the matter in an object is. For example, a box made of steel and a box made of Styrofoam may have the same volume, but their densities will be different. The box of steel will contain more matter and therefore have more mass than the box of Styrofoam. Consequently, the box of steel will have a higher density than the box of Styrofoam. Density is expressed in grams per cubic centimeter and is determined by dividing an object's mass by its volume.

Scientists have determined the density of common substances such as air, water, ice, aluminum, gold, lead, and most of the elements of the periodic table. By figuring out the density of an object, you can determine from what the object is made. However, you must be careful because density can be changed by changing the pressure and/or temperature of an object. Increasing the pressure on an object will always increase the density because it will compact the particles closer together. Increasing the temperature of an object generally will decrease the density with a few exceptions, such as water.

Legend of Archimedes

Mass, volume, and density have been studied since ancient times. The Legend of Archimedes is one of the earliest examples of the use of water displacement. Archimedes was tasked with determining if the King's goldsmith was stealing gold while he was making the King's crown. The King suspected the goldsmith of keeping the gold for himself and replacing it with a much cheaper metal in the crown. Archimedes was puzzled about how best to determine if this was the case. While taking a bath, Archimedes noticed that the water level rose when he sat in the water. He realized that his density could be determined by the amount of water that his body displaced. He decided to compare the displacement of water caused by the amount of gold that should have been used in the crown with the displacement of water caused by the actual crown. By using the theory of water displacement he would be able to determine the goldsmith's guilt or innocence. Upon this discovery, legend has it that Archimedes went running through the streets screaming "Eureka! Eureka!"

Theme/Concept

C3

What is the main idea of the Legend of Archimedes? Justify your answer.

Inference

C2

What inferences can be made about the relationship among mass, volume, and density? Use evidence from the text to support your answer.

Literary Elements

C1

How would you characterize Archimedes? Support your answer with details from the text.

MASS, VOLUME, AND DENSITY

Creative Synthesis

D3

Write a math word problem that uses a formula
for finding volume and/or density.

Summarizing

D2

In three sentences or less, summarize the Legend of Archimedes.

Paraphrasing

D1

In your own words, describe the difference between mass and weight.

MASS, VOLUME, AND DENSITY

Population Explosion:
How Math Helps You Understand America's Past

Do you remember the Mayflower from your American history lessons? This famous ship landed in Massachusetts on November 21, 1620. Thirty-seven Pilgrims and the ship's crew left England on September 16, 1620. How long did it take the passengers to cross the Atlantic Ocean? Once they had landed in the New World, the passengers of the Mayflower settled in Plymouth Rock. Over the next 113 years, the 13 colonies were settled. The thirteen colonies are listed below, in alphabetical order, with their founding dates.

- Connecticut, 1635
- Delaware, 1638
- Georgia, 1733
- Maryland, 1634
- Massachusetts, 1620
- New Hampshire, 1623
- New Jersey, 1660
- New York, 1613
- North Carolina, 1638
- Pennsylvania, 1681
- Rhode Island, 1636
- South Carolina, 1638
- Virginia, 1607

For the first 155 years, the American settlers were under British rule. In the 1770s, the Americans decided they would rather rule themselves. In 1775, the Revolutionary War began when the British tried to destroy guns and ammunitions that the colonists were storing. In 1776, the Declaration of Independence was signed. Finally, in 1783, the American colonists won the Revolutionary War, gaining their freedom from Britain, and officially forming the United States of America. Soon after gaining independence, the United States conducted their first census in 1790. A census is conducted to count the number of people living in a country. Since 1790, the U.S. has conducted a census every 10 years. The graph below shows the results of the 1790 census.

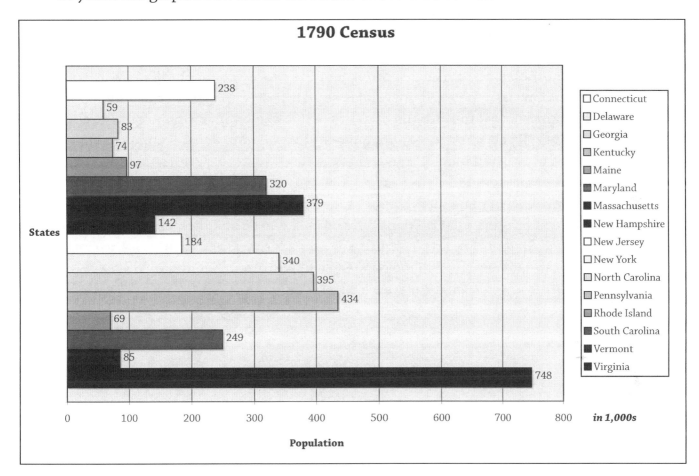

In the early 1800s, the United States began purchasing land to expand the country westward. The Louisiana Purchase in 1803 nearly doubled the land area of America. In the 1840s and 1850s, many people who were living on the east coast decided to move to California on the west coast. Many of these travelers headed west in the pursuit of gold. Gold was discovered in California in 1848 and the Gold Rush began less than a year later. After the Civil War, another large group of people headed west in search of inexpensive land, new job opportunities, and the promise of a better life.

In addition to Americans moving around within the country, there were always more people immigrating, or moving, to the United States. America has always been a nation of immigrants who come from all over the world. Immigration has rapidly increased throughout the years. In 1821, there were less than 500,000 immigrants. In 1991, there were more than 10,000,000.

Between the years of 1892 and 1954, nearly 12 million immigrants passed through Ellis Island, which was the site of the first federal immigration station. Located off the coast of New York, Ellis Island was a convenient location for ships crossing the Atlantic to dock. The passengers would disembark and begin the long process of legally immigrating to the United States. By the 1880s, steam power had been invented, making the journey across the Atlantic shorter and therefore easier. Immigrants came from Europe, the Middle East, the Mediterranean, and Canada. During the peak years of immigration, from 1900 to 1914, nearly 5,000 people arrived at Ellis Island each day. However, the rate of immigration began to decline with the beginning of World War I in 1914. Americans became suspicious of foreigners and the loyalty of immigrants often was questioned. In the 1920s, several laws were passed to control the number of immigrants allowed to enter the States. In 1924, the Immigration Act of 1924 was passed. This law restricted the number of immigrants to a certain percentage of the existing population of a given nationality. This act also restricted the total number of immigrants for the year to 164,000. The Immigration Act of 1924 marked the end of mass immigration to America.

Can you imagine what it might have been like to be an immigrant coming to the United States? How do you think you would feel if you were one of America's earliest settlers watching millions of people move to your country? How has immigration affected what America is like today?

A3

Consequences and Implications

What are the consequences and implications of moving to America either as an early settler or an immigrant?

A2

Cause and Effect

What is the relationship between math and history? Support your answer with evidence from the text.

A1

Sequencing

Sequence the order of the 13 state colony establishments from the first settled to the last settled.

POPULATION EXPLOSION

Creative Synthesis

D3

Use math in some way to represent America's past. Create a relevant map, table, or graph on some dimension of value.

Summarizing

D2

Do you believe the subtitle, "How Math Helps You Understand America's Past," best summarizes the text? Defend your answer.

Paraphrasing

D1

Look at the graph of the 1790 census. If someone couldn't understand how to interpret the graph, how would you explain it to him or her? Write your answer in two or three sentences.

POPULATION EXPLOSION

The Systems of the Human Body: Part I

The human body is made up of different systems that work independently as well as with each other in order for our bodies to function properly. Some of the major body systems are the cardiovascular (kahr-dee-oh-**vas**-kyuh-ler) system, the pulmonary (**puhl**-muh-ner-ee) system, the gastrointestinal (gas-troh-in-**tes**-tuh-nl) system, and the neurological (noor-uh-**loj**-i-kuhl) system. The cardiovascular and pulmonary systems will be discussed in part one of this selection while the gastrointestinal and neurological systems will be discussed in part two.

Cardiovascular System

Also known as the circulatory (**sur**-kyuh-luh-tohr-ee) system, the cardiovascular system is responsible for transporting nutrients, water, and oxygen to all of the cells in your body. This system also carries away waste, like carbon dioxide, that your cells do not need anymore. The cardiovascular system includes your heart, blood, and blood vessels.

The heart is a muscle located slightly to the left of the center of your chest. Its job is to pump blood and keep blood moving throughout your body. Your heart pumps blood through thousands of miles of three types of blood vessels: arteries, capillaries, and veins.

Arteries carry oxygen-rich blood away from the heart to the other cells in your body. Capillaries are thin, tiny blood vessels that connect arteries and veins. They allow nutrients, oxygen, and waste to pass in and out of the blood through their walls. Veins carry blood back to the heart from other cells in the body to get re-oxygenated.

Blood is made up of liquids, solids, and small amounts of gases like oxygen and carbon dioxide. Blood carries nutrients and water to cells and carries waste away from cells. Your blood contains 5 million red blood cells in each drop. It also has white blood cells that fight infections and platelets that stop bleeding. These red blood cells, white blood cells, and platelets are transported throughout the body by a liquid in the blood called *plasma*.

Pulmonary System

Also known as the respiratory (**res**-per-uh-tohr-ee) system, the pulmonary system is made up of the body parts that help you breathe: lungs, trachea (**trey**-kee-uh), bronchi (**brong**-kee), and diaphragm (**dahy**-uh-fram).

The lungs are the main organs of the pulmonary system. They take in oxygen and dispel, or force away, carbon dioxide. Your lungs take up most of the space in your chest; however, your left lung is slightly smaller than your right lung in order to leave enough room for your heart. Within your chest, your lungs are protected by your rib cage. Your lungs work with your circulatory system by providing oxygen for blood. The red blood cells pick up oxygen in the lungs and deliver it to the cells. At the cells, the red blood cells pick up carbon dioxide and bring it back to the lungs, which then expel the carbon dioxide when you exhale, or breathe out.

The trachea, also known as the windpipe, is responsible for filtering the air you breathe before it gets to your lungs. The trachea is covered with tiny cilia (**sill**-ee-uh) that are constantly moving to catch mucus and dust. The trachea extends from the back of your throat to your bronchi in the middle of your chest. The bronchi then branch off into two air tubes, one to the right and one to the left, to deliver air to the lungs.

The diaphragm, another important organ of the pulmonary system, is a dome-shaped muscle beneath your lungs. It is the main muscle used for breathing. When it contracts, it becomes flat, which leaves enough room for your lungs to expand with air when you breathe in. When you exhale, your diaphragm expands, reducing the amount of space for air, which forces the air out of your lungs.

Take a moment to think about what happens with your pulmonary and circulatory systems with each breath you take: your diaphragm contracts, your trachea filters the air you are breathing, your lungs expand, your blood picks up oxygen to deliver to the rest of your cells, your blood drops off carbon dioxide from other cells, your diaphragm expands, and your lungs force out air as you exhale. Now think about how long this whole process takes—less than 6 seconds! Amazing!

Generalizations

B3

Write at least three generalizations about the role of blood in the functioning of your circulatory system.

Classifications

B2

Look at your list. Classify each part by where it is located on your body.
You may not use a miscellaneous or other category.
Then, label each category as close to the heart or far from the heart.

Details

B1

Think about your blood delivering oxygen to your cells. List as many different parts of your body as you can in 2 minutes.

THE SYSTEMS OF THE HUMAN BODY: PART I

Creative Synthesis

D3

Imagine you are a red blood cell. Write a detailed description of your journey through the body. Be specific and use details from the text to support your answer.

Summarizing

D2

In five sentences or less, summarize what happens in both the circulatory and pulmonary systems when you inhale, or take a breath.

Paraphrasing

D1

Rewrite the following statement in your own words: "Your lungs take up most of the space in your chest; however, your left lung is slightly smaller than your right lung in order to leave enough room for your heart."

THE SYSTEMS OF THE HUMAN BODY: PART I

Name: _____ Date: _____

The Systems of the Human Body: Part II

The previous selection discussed the circulatory and pulmonary systems. The second part of "The Systems of the Human Body" will focus on the gastrointestinal (gas-troh-in-**tes**-t*uh*-nl) and neurological (n*oor-uh*-**loj**-i-k*uh*l) systems.

Gastrointestinal System

Also known as the digestive (di-**jes**-tiv) system, the gastrointestinal system converts the food you eat into energy by breaking food down into small pieces of nutrients that your body can absorb into your bloodstream. When you chew, your teeth break food apart, saliva softens it, and your tongue helps push food into your throat during swallowing. Other major organs of the gastrointestinal system are the esophagus (ee-**sof**-*uh*-g*uh*s), the stomach, the small intestine, and the large intestine.

The esophagus is a muscular tube that begins at the back of your throat and connects to your stomach. It helps squeeze food down into your stomach. Your stomach is a J-shaped sack that receives food. The stomach sits just below your heart. Once food arrives in your stomach, the stomach begins to make acids and enzymes (**ĕn**-zīmz) that break food down into a semi-liquid paste while the stomach muscles move the food around. Once you swallow food, it stays in your stomach for approximately 2 hours.

When it is time for food to leave your stomach the semi-liquid food paste moves into your small intestine. The small intestine is a 20–25-foot-long tube that is coiled in your abdomen (a medical term for your lower stomach). The center of your small intestine is directly below your belly button. While the partially digested food travels through your small intestine, vitamins, minerals, carbohydrates, fats, and proteins are absorbed by finger-like structures called villi (**vil**-ahy) and sent to your bloodstream.

Any leftovers that are not absorbed during the journey through the small intestine enter your large intestine. The large intestine is approximately 5 feet long and also coiled in your abdomen. Along with your colon, which is part of your large intestine, your large intestine turns the semi-liquid paste into solid waste by removing all of the water. Solid waste collects in the rectum (**rek**-t*uh*m) and leaves the body as feces (**fee**-seez) during a bowel movement.

Neurological System

Also known as the nervous system, the neurological system is the control and communications center for your body. It sends and receives messages as well as controls all your thoughts and movements. The main components of the neurological systems are neurons, brain, and spinal cord.

The cells of the neurological system are called *neurons*. Neurons carry electrical messages around the brain and to the nerves throughout your body. When you are born, you have all the neurons you will ever need. However, they are not connected to each other. When you learn and practice things, your brain starts to create pathways that connect different neurons. Over time, these neuron connections make the things you learn easier to do and more automatic.

Your brain is the main information center for your body. Billions of neurons sending and receiving electrical messages help the brain respond to input from the five senses—hearing, smelling, seeing, touching, and tasting. These neurons also help the brain process thoughts. These functions occur in three main areas of the brain: cerebrum, cerebellum, and brain stem. The cerebrum is the largest part of the brain. It is responsible for thinking, processing input from your senses, and for any movements that you control (such as reaching for a glass, walking down the sidewalk, or smiling at a friend). The cerebellum is responsible for balance and coordination. The brain stem, which is linked to the spinal cord, controls digestion, breathing, your heartbeat—in other words, all the actions your body does automatically. The brain stem controls those actions that you do not have to think about and over which you do not have control.

The spinal cord is a tube of neurons that is attached to your brain stem and runs along your spine. Nerves branch out all over your body from the spinal cord. Information travels from the nerves to the spinal cord, up the spinal cord, and into the brain to be processed. Messages also are sent from the brain to the rest of your body through the spinal cord and nerves.

Consequences and Implications

A3

What would be the consequences if your gastrointestinal system was not working properly? Use evidence from the text to support your answer.

Cause and Effect

A2

What is the effect of food entering your stomach?

Sequencing

A1

Describe, in order, the steps of the digestive process from the time food enters your mouth.

THE SYSTEMS OF THE HUMAN BODY: PART II

Theme/Concept

C3

What is the overall theme of this selection? Write a new title that better represents the theme. Justify your answer.

Inference

C2

What inferences can you make about the importance of nerves to the neurological system? Use evidence from the text to support your answer.

Literary Elements

C1

The neurological system has been characterized as the control and communications center of the body. Describe this characterization. Use details from the text to support your answer.

THE SYSTEMS OF THE HUMAN BODY: PART II

What Is Sound?

We all hear sound every day. But, have you ever stopped to think about what sound really is? Sound is a form of energy that travels as waves and causes a vibration of individual molecules—the smallest particles of substances—within a solid, liquid, or gas. When the molecules crowd together, there is compression. When the molecules spread apart, there is rarefaction. A series of alternating compressions and rarefactions makes sound waves. The properties of sound waves include wavelength, period, pitch, amplitude, frequency, and speed.

Wavelength is the horizontal distance between two equivalent points on a sound wave. Imagine you are looking at waves in the ocean. The wavelength is the distance between the top of one wave to the top of the next wave. It is the same with sound—from the top of one sound wave to the top of the next sound wave is the wavelength.

Period is the time it takes for one complete cycle of the wave to pass a designated point. In other words, period is the time it takes sound to travel the distance of one wavelength. Typically, a longer period indicates a lower pitch.

Pitch is a characteristic of musical sound. It refers to highness or lowness of a musical note. Think about the keys of a piano. At the far left end of the piano, the keys have a very low sound, or pitch. The sound waves from the strings attached to these keys have long periods or distances between wavelengths. At the opposite end of the piano, the keys have a very high sound, or pitch. These strings have shorter periods and distances between wavelengths.

Amplitude is the height of each sound wave. A loud sound is produced by a high wave or a wave with high amplitude. A soft sound is produced by shorter waves with smaller amplitudes. Amplitude is measured in decibels, which measures the intensity of the sound. If you amplify a sound, or increase its intensity, then you also increase its volume.

Frequency is the number of vibrations—compressions and rarefactions—that occur in one second. Frequency is measured in hertz. Therefore, 900 hertz is the equivalent of 900 vibrations per second. In music, the different frequencies of sound waves are classified as different tones.

The speed of sound waves varies depending on the medium—solid, liquid, or gas—through which it is traveling. Sound travels slowest through gas, faster through liquids, and fastest through solids. With gas such as air, temperature affects the speed at which sound can move through it. The colder the temperature, the faster sound moves because the molecules are closer together, which makes compressions and rarefactions more likely to occur. In liquids, sound moves faster because the molecules are already closer together. In fact, sound can move four times faster through water than through air. Therefore, it seems logical that sound will move faster through solids because the molecules are even closer together. Sound moves 17 times faster through steel than it does through air.

Another interesting characteristic of sound waves is that they travel in the same direction until another energy force or object gets in the way and reflects the sound. Have you ever heard an echo? An echo is caused by sound waves that are not absorbed but rather are reflected back to their source.

Name: _____ Date: _____

Generalizations

B3

Write at least three generalizations about sound.

Classifications

B2

Classify the list you made into categories. You may not use a miscellaneous or other category.

Details

B1

Take two minutes to sit quietly and listen. Make a list of all the different sounds you hear.

WHAT IS SOUND?

Theme/Concept

C3

In no more than one sentence, write the main idea of this text.

Inference

C2

What evidence supports the different speeds that sound passes through different mediums such as liquids, solids, and gases? Use details from the text to support your answer.

Literary Elements

C1

How would you describe sound to someone who is deaf and has never heard sound before? Be sure to use plenty of details in your explanation.

WHAT IS SOUND?

Pre- and Postassessments and Exemplars

Appendix A contains the pre- and postassessment readings and answer forms, as well as a rubric for scoring the assessments. The preassessment should be administered before any work with *Jacob's Ladder* is conducted. After all readings and questions have been answered, the postassessment can be given to track student improvement on the ladder skill sets. Included in this appendix are example answers for both the pre- and postassessments. The answers are taken from student responses given during the piloting of this curriculum.

Fifth-Grade Pretest:
Emily Dickinson Poem

Please read the poem by Emily Dickinson below. Answer the four questions related to the poem.

> This is my letter to the world,
> That never wrote to me,—
> The simple news that Nature told,
> With tender majesty.
>
> Her message is committed
> To hands I cannot see;
> For love of her, sweet countrymen,
> Judge tenderly of me!

1. What does the author think about the world? Provide evidence from the story to defend your answer.

   _____

   _____

   _____

   _____

   _____

   _____

2. What did the author mean when she wrote, "The simple news that Nature told with tender Majesty"? Provide evidence from the story to defend your answer.

   _____

   _____

   _____

   _____

   _____

   _____

3. What do you think this poem is about? Give a reason why you think so.

_____

_____

_____

_____

_____

_____

4. Create a title for this poem. Give a reason why your title is appropriate for this poem.

_____

_____

_____

_____

_____

_____

Fifth-Grade Posttest:
Emily Dickinson Poem

Please read the poem by Emily Dickinson below. Then answer the four questions related to the poem.

There is no frigate like a book
To take us lands away,
Nor any coursers like a page
Of prancing poetry.
This traverse may the poorest take
Without oppress of toll;
How frugal is the chariot
That bears a human soul!

1. What does the author think about books? Provide evidence from the story to defend your answer.

_____

_____

_____

_____

_____

_____

2. A frigate is a small warship. Why does the author compare a book to a frigate? Provide evidence from the story to defend your answer.

_____

_____

_____

_____

_____

_____

3. What one word best describes what this poem is about? Give a reason why you think so.

_____

_____

_____

_____

_____

_____

4. Create a title for this poem. Give a reason why your title is appropriate for this poem.

_____

_____

_____

_____

_____

_____

Name: _____

Date: _____

Assessment Scoring Rubric

Question	Points				
	0	1	2	3	4
1 Implications and Consequences (Ladder A)	Provides no response or response is inappropriate to the task demand	Limited, vague, inaccurate; rewords the prompt or copies from text	Response is accurate and makes sense but does not adequately address all components of the question or provide rationale from text	Response is accurate; answers all parts of the question; provides a rationale that justifies answer	Response is well written, specific, insightful; answers all parts of the questions, offers substantial support, and incorporates evidence from the text
2 Inference (Ladder C)	Provides no response or response is inappropriate to the task demand	Limited, vague, inaccurate; rewords the prompt or copies from text	Accurate response but literal interpretation with no support from the text	Interpretive response with limited support from the text	Insightful, interpretive, well-written response with substantial support from the text
3 Theme/ Generalization (Ladders B and C)	Provides no response or response is inappropriate to the task demand	Limited, vague, inaccurate; rewords the prompt or copies from text	Literal description of the story without explaining the theme; no reasons why	Valid, interpretive response with limited reasoning from the text	Insightful, interpretive response with substantial justification or reasoning
4 Creative Synthesis (Ladder D)	Provides no response or response is inappropriate to the task demand	Limited, vague, inaccurate; rewords the prompt or copies from text	Appropriate but literal title with no attempt to support	Interpretive title with limited reasoning or justification	Insightful title, interpretive, and extensive justification or reasoning

 Jacob's Ladder Reading Comprehension Program, Level 3 © Prufrock Press • This page may be photocopied or reproduced with permission for classroom use.

Example Answers

Fifth-Grade Pretest: Emily Dickinson Poem

Note. These answers are based on student responses and teacher ratings from field trials conducted by the Center for Gifted Education. The answers have not been changed from the original student response.

1. **What does the author think about the world? Provide evidence from the story to defend your answer.**

   1-point responses might include:

   - The author thinks the world can write.

   - The world doesn't like her.

   - She thinks that no one wrote her back.

   2-point responses might include:

   - I think the author feels good about the world and the way it looks.

   - I think the author thinks the world is graceful, beautiful, and majestic.

   - She loves the earth and everything on it.

   3-point responses might include:

   - She thinks the world is majestic because it says: "The simple news that nature told with tender majesty."

   - The author thinks the world is nice. I think this because she called the world (nature) tender (soft).

   4-point responses might include:

   - What the author thinks of the world is that nature sends a message. I know this because it says "The simple news that nature told."

   - The author thinks the world knows what she's like inside because it said in the poem "To hands I cannot see."

   - I think the author thinks the world is a place to be free because the author can express his or her feelings and write a "letter to the world."

2. **What did the author mean when she wrote "The simple news that Nature told with tender majesty"? Provide evidence from the story to defend your answer.**

1-point responses might include:

- The author means that the world is filled with tender majesty.
- Nature told her thank you.
- Nature was happy.

2-point responses might include:

- I think the author meant that nature was trying to tell her something.
- The author meant that nature tells a story softly and gently.
- She means that people should treat the forests with care.

3-point responses might include:

- I think the author meant that nature told the author a kind message, because tender means kind.
- The author meant that nature was answering her letter and sharing news. She meant that nature was beautiful because if something is majestic that usually means it is beautiful.
- I think she meant the world was good because tender majesty makes me think of a "soft world."

4-point responses might include:

- The author meant that Nature's news was weather because "The simple news" is the rain and snow. Weather can be tender, like soft snow.
- I think it means that nature has shared news with the author. Nature can't speak or write therefore nature has never written to the author but given her news in other ways.
- I think "The simple news that Nature told with tender majesty" means nature is sharing sad news. Because the line "her message is committed" makes the news seem important and the line "for love of her sweet countrymen" sounds like the news is sad.

3. What do you think this poem is about? Give a reason why you think so.

1-point responses might include:

- I think this poem is about what the author thinks about the world.
- It's about sending a letter to the world.
- Nature, that's what it talks about the most.

2-point responses might include:

- I think this poem is about how much the author loves the world because she is talking about how beautiful the world is.
- It is about the world because it talks about nature.
- I think this poem is about nature and its message.

3-point responses might include:

- I think it is about how nature relies on people.
- I think it is about the freedom to say what you think.
- This poem is about Mother Nature and the story she tells.

4-point responses might include:

- I think this poem is about a girl who wants to know what the world thinks of her because at the end of the poem she says "Judge tenderly of me."
- I think this poem is about a relative who past away because it said "to hands I can not see." The news that nature told is sad news of a death.
- This poem is about telling the world about pollution but no one will listen. "The simple news nature told me" is Mother Nature is being polluted and so the author is telling the world to stop.

4. Create a title for this poem. Give a reason why your title is appropriate for this poem.

1-point responses might include:

- World
- Here's a Letter because the poem is a letter.
- To: World From: Me

2-point responses might include:

- I think The World would be a good title because the whole poem talks about the world.

- My Letter to the World would be a good title because the poem is about someone writing a letter to the world.

- The title should be Nature because the whole poem is about nature.

3-point responses might include:

- The Poem of Love, because it is a touching and sweet poem.

- Majestic World is a good title because one of the lines says "The simple news that nature told, with tender majesty." So this line shows that the author thinks the world is majestic.

- Nature's Message would be a good title because the author talks about nature "talking" to her.

4-point responses might include:

- My title is World Peace. I think it's a good title because the author tells about how tender and sweet the world is. The author says "For love of her" showing that people should protect the world.

- I would name this poem The Message that Never Got Sent because it sounds like the author is trying to tell the world a message about nature but no one is listening.

- The World Should Know. I think this would be a good title because the poem is a letter about what the author thinks is important. The author wants to share what she knows about nature.

Example Answers

Fifth-Grade Posttest: Emily Dickinson Poem

Note. These answers are based on student responses and teacher ratings from field trials conducted by the Center for Gifted Education. The answers have not been changed from the original student response.

1. **What does the author think about books? Provide evidence from the poem to defend your answer.**

   1-point responses might include:

   - The author thinks there is no frigate like a book. This evidence is in the first sentence first paragraph.
   - She thinks that books are a frigate which might mean warship.
   - The author thinks books are fun and good.

   2-point responses might include:

   - The author thinks books are like nothing else. I think that because the author says books are not like frigates or courses.
   - She thinks highly of books because she said "There is no frigate like a book" which means she that she likes books a whole lot.
   - I think the author likes books because she compared a lot of things to them.

   3-point responses might include:

   - She thinks books are just like frigates because they take you lands away.
   - The author loves books. I know this because during the poem she talks about how books can give you stories you can think up in your imagination.
   - The author thinks that books take you to different places and are good because she says "There is no frigate like a book" and "Nor courses like a page."

   4-point responses might include:

   - Emily Dickinson thinks books are a good way of learning and there are many places to borrow them, like a library where you don't have to pay. I know this because she said "This traverse may the poorest take without oppress of toll."

- I think the author likes books and really gets into them because she said "there is no frigate like a book to take us lands away." Also, I think she believes every page counts and that they can take you dashing through the story or poem because she said "nor any courses like a page of prancing poetry."

- The author thinks that books can take your mind to distant places without ever leaving your home. I think this because of the sentence from the author's poem: "There is no frigate like a book to take us lands away."

2. A frigate is a small warship. Why does the author compare a book to a frigate? Provide evidence from the story to defend your answer.

1-point responses might include:

- Some books have warships in them.

- They are two things you can see.

- She is comparing a frigate to a book. She said that there is no frigate like a book.

2-point responses might include:

- The author is comparing a book to a frigate because she thinks they are the same.

- She compares a frigate to a book because to her a book is a small warship.

- The author compares a book to a warship because she likes books as much as a small warship.

3-point responses might include:

- She compares the two because when she says "To take us lands away," she means that a book is like a warship. A ship is a form of transportation and a book can make your mind think about the place you are reading about.

- I think the author compared a book to a frigate because she said a book goes to far lands and a frigate travels to lands far away.

- The author compares a book to a frigate because they both bear a human's soul.

4-point responses might include:

- The author compares a frigate to a book because a frigate is small so it can deliver soldiers to far away places and a book can take our imaginations to far away places.

- I think she is trying to say that a book can be powerful, even more powerful than a warship. In the poem she says "There is no frigate like a book to take us lands away, Nor any course like a page."

- She compares a book to a frigate because you can travel to say, Antarctica, just by opening a book. A frigate can also take you to different countries, but it might take hours.

3. **What one word best describes what this poem is about? Give a reason why you think so.**

1-point responses might include:

- Frigate

- Like

- Neat, because it talks about warships and she uses big and new words.

2-point responses might include:

- Books, because she pretty much talks just about books in her story.

- War! This one word describes the poem because the poem said there is "no frigate like a book."

- The word I pick is amazing because it is so powerful.

3-point responses might include:

- Books, because the author explains why she loves books so much and tells what happens when she reads different kinds of book. She tells what happens in her imagination.

- Joys would be the one word that best describes what this poem is about. I chose that word because the poem says that books and poetry are really good.

- Read, I think that because she promotes reading throughout the entire poem.

4-point responses might include:

- The one word that best describes what the poem is about is imaginative. I think this because she thinks books take you to mystic places.
- Relaxing, I chose relaxing because when you read this poem it makes you want to grab a book and get comfortable.
- Magic, I think that the poem is about the magic of reading. I think that because it talks about where a book can take you.

4. Create a title for this poem. Give a reason why your title is appropriate for this poem.

1-point responses might include:

- A book. It talks about books.
- Books and Warships
- A Poem about Books

2-point responses might include:

- I think a good title for this story might be War because it talks about warships.
- A Book. It talks about books.
- Frigate. This is a good name for it because he talks about a frigate.

3-point responses might include:

- I think a good title for this poem is Books because it compares books to other things.
- Read to Find is the title I would pick. I think this because you find out things when you read.
- Read a Book. This title says a lot about the poem, because the author encourages you to read in this poem.

4-point responses might include:

- The Magic of Words. I think it is good because the poem talks about books being magical, taking you to magical places.
- I think The Joy of Reading would be a good title because she talks about enjoying reading in this poem.

- A good title would be All Around the World with a Book. I think this because the poem talks about the many places around the world you can go by reading.

Record-Keeping Forms/ Documents

Appendix B contains three record-keeping forms and documents:

1. *Brainstorming/Answer Sheet*: This should be given to students for completion after reading a selection so that they may jot ideas or questions about the selection they read prior to participating in discussion. The purpose of this sheet is to capture students' thoughts and ideas generated after individually reading a text. This sheet serves as a guide for student preparedness so that the student is ready to share ideas in group discussion.

2. *Reflection Page*: This form may be completed by the student after group or class discussion on the readings. The reflection page is designed as a metacognitive approach to help students reflect on their strengths and weaknesses and to promote process skills. After discussion, students use the reflection page to record new ideas that were generated by others' comments and ideas.

3. *Classroom Diagnostic Form*: This form is for teachers and is designed to aid them in keeping track of the progress and skill mastery of their students. With this chart, teachers can record student progress in relation to each ladder skill within a genre and select additional ladders and story selections based on student needs.

Brainstorming/Answer Sheet

Use this form to brainstorm thoughts and ideas about the readings and ladder questions before discussing with a partner.

Circle One: A3 B3 C3 D3

Circle One: A2 B2 C2 D2

Circle One: A1 B1 C1 D1

Selection Title: _____

Name: _____ Date: _____

Jacob's Ladder Reading Comprehension Program, Level 3 © Prufrock Press • This page may be photocopied or reproduced with permission for classroom use.

Name: _____   Date: _____

My Reflection on
Today's Reading and Discussion

Selection Title: _____

What I did well:

_____

_____

_____

_____

What I learned:

_____

_____

_____

_____

New ideas I have after discussion:

_____

_____

_____

_____

Next time I need to:

_____

_____

_____

_____

Classroom Diagnostic Form

Short Stories

Use this document to record student completion of ladder sets with the assessment of work.

0 = Needs Improvement   1 = Satisfactory   2 = Exceeds Expectations

Student Name	Brazilian Paradise		Christa McAuliffe		The Competition		Excerpts From Common Sense		Franklin D. Roosevelt's First Inaugural Address		The Gettysburg Address		Legacy		Moving Pictures Evoke Concern, 1922		Washington's Letter to His Wife Martha		Why Own a House When You Can Own an R.V.?	
	A	B	A	C	C	D	B	C	B	D	C	D	B	D	A	D	A	C	B	C

 Jacob's Ladder Reading Comprehension Program, Level 3 © Prufrock Press • This page may be photocopied or reproduced with permission for classroom use.

Classroom Diagnostic Form
Poetry

Use this document to record student completion of ladder sets with the assessment of work.

0 = Needs Improvement   1 = Satisfactory   2 = Exceeds Expectations

Student Name	A Corn-Song		The Harp			I Am the Moon			If		The Lament of the Frog Prince			The Road Not Taken		Sinking Sunset			Sunset			The Visit		A Winter Morning	
	A	D	B	C	B	C	C	D	A	C	A	C	A	C	B	C	A	B	A	B

Classroom Diagnostic Form

Nonfiction

Use this document to record student completion of ladder sets with the assessment of work.

0 = Needs Improvement   1 = Satisfactory   2 = Exceeds Expectations

Student Name	Economics 101		Mass, Volume, and Density		Population Explosion		Systems of the Human Body: Part I		Systems of the Human Body: Part II		What Is Sound?	
	A	D	C	D	A	D	B	D	A	C	B	C

Answer Key

This key includes example answers for all ladder questions. Sample answers were generated to illustrate the skills students should be mastering. However, because the questions are open-ended and designed to promote discussion, these answers should only be used as a guide. Variations and original thought should be valued and rewarded.

Short Stories Answer Set

These are suggested answers only. Answers will vary.

Brazilian Paradise

Ladder Set A

A1. The author moved to Brasilia; the author's family lived in an undeveloped area of the country; the author saw monkeys; the author explored the jungle around her home with her family; the author gained a greater appreciation for the beauty of nature.

A2. The first area of Brazil the family saw was devoid of nature because it had been developed by people who wanted to start businesses and/or sell houses as a means to make money.

A3. Increased commercialization would cause more and more of the Brazilian nature to be destroyed. A greater area of land would become devoid of nature.

Ladder Set B

B1. Answers will vary. Some examples might include: shimmering lakes; colorful flowering trees; leaf-cutter ants; no humidity; brief rain showers; skittering, playful monkeys.

B2. Answers will vary. Some examples using the list above might include: natural flora; natural fauna; jungle wildlife; climate.

B3. Answers will vary. An example using the list and categories above might be: "Brasilia nature is colorful."

Christa McAuliffe: A Teacher on Earth and in Space!

Ladder Set A

A1. The temperature dropped, making the weather cold; the primary and secondary O-rings on the Challenger became stiff because of the cold; the primary and secondary O-rings did not form an airtight seal; the Challenger launched; the hot gases burned through the primary O-ring; the secondary O-ring was not in a position to stop the gases from burning through the outer casing of the solid rocket booster; fire burned through the external tank; fuel spilled out; the Challenger ignited and exploded 73 seconds after launching.

A2. She wanted to teach in space because she wanted to get the most out of life as possible and to try new things. She also wanted to have an impact on others and to choose to do things in her life that would have an impact on her.

A3. There might have been more teachers who went into space; the space/education program might have been extended and students might enjoy many lessons from space; the space program might have been revitalized by what it had to offer education.

Ladder Set D

D1. Yes. She was very brave to take advantage of an opportunity to do something new and exciting. She wanted to go into space in order to enhance the education of students on Earth. She was not afraid to try something new and to "seize the day."

D2. Yes. The O-rings could have been checked before the Challenger launched. The scientists might have thought the cold weather might affect the O-rings.

D3. The author addresses bravery through the way she describes how Christa McAuliffe lived her life rather than dwelling on how McAuliffe died. The author talks about Christa's bravery for wanting to do something new and different and calls her a hero because of what she wanted to do in the name of education.

The Competition

Ladder Set C

C1. Answers will vary. Examples might include nervousness, confidence, calm. Support for these emotions: her palms were sweaty and her heart was racing while she was listening to the ninth performer; she was confident in her ability to play her piece beautifully and well; once she began playing her violin she was calm and no longer worried about the other performer's ability.

C2. Yes, she did deserve to win. She was confident in her playing ability, but she was not cocky. She acknowledged the ninth player's ability and realized she was going to have to put on a great performance if she was going to win. She also played to the best of her ability and was proud of herself before she knew she had won.

C3. It doesn't matter whether you win or lose, but that you do your best.

Ladder Set D

D1. She is thinking about what a great performer the ninth player is and is starting to doubt her own ability. Her concentration on her piece is broken and she begins to wonder if she will be able to win the competition. Her heart is beating very fast and her palms are sweaty—for the first time since the competition began she was nervous.

D2. The author was pleased with her place in the program. As she listened to the performers, she became convinced that she would definitely win because she was so much better than the other players. Then the ninth player performed and the author began to wonder if she could win the competition. Having been humbled by the ninth player's performance, the author focused on her performance rather than on winning. She truly tried her best and, as a result, won the competition.

D3. Answers will vary. Students should include a description of the ninth player, what he felt and/or thought while the others were performing, specifically while the author was playing, and how the ninth player felt when he didn't win.

Excerpts From *Common Sense*

Ladder Set B

B1. Answers will vary. Some examples might include: by selling our goods to countries other than England; by asserting our independence; by arguing that we are bigger than the "primary planet"; by claiming Europe as our parent country rather than England.

B2. Answers will vary. Some categories based on the above examples might be asserting independence; seeking alternative trade markets.

B3. Answers will vary. An example based on the above categories and list might be, "A nation should be self-reliant."

Ladder Set C

C1. During the time he lived, Thomas Paine was a progressive man. He was willing to resist the power being exerted over America by England because he could foresee a better future when America and England would coexist as equal nations. Paine was willing to both believe America was capable of being an independent nation, as well as to speak up for America's independence.

C2. America can have alliances with countries other than England; Europe is the true parent nation; America is physically bigger than the island trying to exert her power; England does not respect America.

C3. Answers will vary. An example might be, "A nation's freedom is exhibited by its ability to sustain itself."

Franklin D. Roosevelt's First Inaugural Address (Excerpt)

Ladder Set B

B1. Answers will vary. Some examples might include: recognize that material wealth is not the standard of success; end dishonest practices in banks and business; be honest; have self-respect; and realize we cannot only take, but must also give.

B2. Answers will vary. Some examples based on the list above might include: positive feelings about oneself; helping others; reevaluating priorities.

B3. Answers will vary. An example based on the list and categories above might be, "Self respect is more valuable than material possessions."

Ladder Set D

D1. The effort and result of hard work is more valuable than money.

D2. Roosevelt told the American people that he knew their spirits were low and that they were struggling to survive. But, that these hard times will pass. Americans should not lose respect for themselves and others; they should help their neighbors. Americans should place their value in something other than material possessions and should not lose faith in America.

D3. Answers will vary. Student responses should be in the format of an essay or a letter and should be address Roosevelt's optimistic outlook on life during the Great Depression.

The Gettysburg Address

Ladder Set C

C1. The soldiers who died during the Battle of Gettysburg gave their lives for their country; should be honored for what they did while living rather than for the fact they died; that the living cannot allow them to have died in vain; that the living must dedicate the rest of their lives to continuing the work the soldiers had begun.

C2. Lincoln was hopeful for the future of America; he believed the American people would do what was right for the country; that America would have a "new birth of freedom"; and that "government of the people, by the people, for the people, shall not perish."

C3. Answers will vary. Examples include: "Liberty is worth fighting for" and "Liberty should be one of a nation's most treasured gifts."

Ladder Set D

D1. Those of us who have not died in the war should continue to fight for the liberty for which the brave soldiers died.

D2. Freedom and liberty are of utmost importance to this country; important enough for many brave men to die while protecting them. It is the responsibility of those citizens still living to honor these men's lives by continuing to fight for the cause.

D3. Answers will vary. Stories should refer to the identity of the stakeholder and his or her emotional reaction to "The Gettysburg Address."

Legacy

Ladder Set B

B1. Answers will vary. Examples might include: his generosity; his storytelling ability; his love of education; his dedication to his family.

B2. Answers will vary. Examples based on the list above include: education, memories, and family.

B3. Answers will vary. An example might be, "Family should be one's first priority."

Ladder Set D

D1. Uncle Charlie loved going to school and loved learning. However, when his father died from the flu, Uncle Charlie realized he was now the "man of the family." He also realized he could not support his family and continue to go to school. He decided it was more important to him for his sisters to finish school and for his family to be able to eat than for him to finish school. (Students also might choose to include a description of where Uncle Charlie went to school and what attending the one room schoolhouse might have been like.)

D2. The author remembers Uncle Charlie most for the stories he told and for the pride he showed in the author's academic success. The author remembers the times Uncle Charlie sent her a small reward for doing well in school and for the way Uncle Charlie wouldn't let the author miss school while Uncle Charlie was dying. The author also remembers how Uncle Charlie always put his family first. The author wants to show her love for her family by paying tribute to Uncle Charlie in this essay.

D3. Answers will vary. Students' responses should be an essay written from Uncle Charlie's point of view or in the format of a letter from Uncle Charlie to the author.

Moving Pictures Evoke Concern, 1922

Ladder Set A

A1. Paragraph 1: Motion pictures are a great invention that can be educational and are accessible by all.

Paragraph 2: Through motion pictures, people can learn about places they may never be able to visit.

Paragraph 3: However, the motion pictures have been corrupted.

Paragraph 4: Motion pictures should be regulated and should not provide a bad example for people.

Paragraph 5: Characters in motion pictures will be role models and, therefore, should be good role models.

A2. Yes, because the criminals in movies serve as role models for young people who do not have live role models in their lives. The "young criminals" get their ideas on the "romance of crime" from the movies.

A3. By allowing movies to remain uncensored, they will continue to portray negative role models for those watching them, according to Myers. Answers will vary regarding the consequences if movies were censored; a sample answer might be that if movies were censored then all movies would portray the role models deemed appropriate by those in charge of censoring the movies.

Ladder Set D

D1. Motion pictures can have characters that serve as role models for how to act with honesty, to be kind to others, and work hard for what you want.

D2. Movies will affect people and how they act. Those in charge of making movies should act responsibly and provide good role models for viewers.

D3. Answers will vary. The format should have the tone of a speech, should focus on movies and young people, and should be limited to a page.

Washington's Letter to His Wife Martha

Ladder Set A

A1. Paragraph 1: Washington tells his wife he will be leading the army.

Paragraph 2: Washington talks about his own uneasiness in being given this position.

Paragraph 3: Washington tells his wife he understands it is his duty to serve his country in this manner.

Washington chose this order for his letter because he wanted to be honest with his wife about his true feelings regarding his new position. Although he realizes leading the army is his duty to his nation, he knows his wife will understand his trepidation about taking over this role.

A2. Answers will vary. Examples might include: His wife will miss Washington and worry about his safety. She also will have to take care of things at home by herself.

A3. Answers will vary. An example might include: If Washington had refused to lead the army, the morale of the soldiers might have been negatively impacted and the war might not have been won by America.

Ladder Set C

C1. George Washington was a brave, patriotic man. He was willing to lead an army into battle for an unknown length of time. He was willing to leave his wife and take a position he was not very excited about taking just because he knew his country needed him.

C2. Yes, he does because he loves his country and wants to support the cause of the war. No, he doesn't because he does not want to leave his wife and he is worried about his ability to successfully lead the army.

C3. Washington's letter to his wife addresses the concept of honor through Washington's willingness to leave his wife and to lead the army because of his dedication to his nation. The honorable thing to do was to accept the position even though it was not something he would have voluntarily chosen to do.

Why Own a House When You Can Own an R.V.?

Ladder Set B

B1. Answers will vary. Examples might include: soccer practice, music lessons, school, work, visiting grandparents, cleaning the house, mowing the lawn, games.

B2. Answers will vary. Some categories based on the examples above might include: athletics, family, education, and work.

B3. Answers will vary. Based on the examples above, one might include: "Families tend to overschedule themselves."

Ladder Set C

C1. Answers will vary. Student responses should include the elements of a busy family life.

C2. Answers will vary. Student responses could agree or disagree with the author's position and must include evidence from the text to support his or her answer.

C3. Time is limited; time should be used wisely; family time is overscheduled.

Poetry Answer Set

These are suggested answers only. Answers will vary.

A Corn-Song

Ladder Set A

A1. Master is: sitting on the porch; thinking; dreaming
Slaves are: Returning from working in the fields; walking slowly; singing.

A2. Answers may vary, but may include:
Cause/Effect
Sun going down/purple light
Hard work and tired from working in the field all day/slaves returning slowly
They are tired/heavy tread
They are proud/light of heart and high of head
Hard work/halting steps, slow and weary

A3. The end of the day for the master is a time of relaxation and dreaming and planning. The end of the day for the slaves is a time to rest from the hard work of the day.

Ladder Set D

D1. Students should rewrite the first stanza in their own words. Answers will vary but should include: at the end of the day the master is relaxing and dreaming.

D2. Students should use their own words to explain what is happening in the poem. Answers should include: while the master is relaxing, the slaves are returning from a hard day of work.

D3. Students will compose a poem using this poem for a model. They will use a teacher and students at the end of the day for the characters. They should include a refrain that is sung by the students.

The Harp

Ladder Set B

B1. Answers will vary. Students are to generate a list of disabilities. Lists may include the following: paralyzed, AD/HD, blind, deaf.

B2. Answers will vary. Students are to categorize the list from Activity B1 and create a title for each category. Categories could include physical and mental.

B3. Answers will vary. Students are to create at least three generalizations about the examples from Activity B2. An example may be: Disabilities can affect you physically and/or mentally.

Ladder Set C

C1. Answers will vary. Students should use a graphic organizer, such as a web, to describe Caroline. Some adjectives may include dedicated, young, blind, and musician.

C2. Answers will vary. Students should create a list of character traits for Caroline. They should write a word or phrase from the poem to support each descriptor.

C3. Answers will vary. Students should get the idea that just because someone has a disability, it does not mean they are unable to do other things well. The author may have told this story to encourage those with disabilities to work on their strengths. Students should write a paragraph stating their opinions and support these opinions with words and phrases from the poem.

I Am the Moon

Ladder Set B

B1. Answers will vary, but should include:

- the moon is pale
- there is only one moon
- the stars surround the moon
- the moon is paler than it was in the past
- when the sun comes up, the moon goes away

B2. Answers will vary. Students should classify the statements listed in Activity B1. They should create a title for each group.

B3. Answers will vary. Students will create three generalizations using evidence from the poem. Example: The moon does not shine as bright as it used to.

Ladder Set C

C1. Create a T-Chart. Answers will vary, but may include:

Imagery	Sense
single, pale, lifeless eye	sight
star strewn cloak	sight
drowned out by our city lights and smoke	sight

C2. Students should use the imagery from the poem and write a description of the moon. Answers will vary.

C3. Answers will vary. Students will create a poem of their own that uses imagery.

If

Ladder Set C

C1. Answers will vary. Students should make a list of words and phrases that describe the military leader. Some adjectives are: calm, trustworthy, and confident.

C2. Answers will vary. Students should use the examples from the text to prove each description word or phrase from their list in Activity C1. For example, Calm: ". . . keep your head when all about you are losing theirs."

C3. Answers may vary, but students should get the sense that the theme of the poem is "how to be successful in life."

Ladder Set D

D1. Answers will vary. Students will choose one stanza to rewrite in their own words.

D2. Answers will vary. Students will write one or two sentences to summarize the stanza chosen in Activity D1.

D3. Answers will vary. Students will choose an occupation and create an 8-line poem, using "If" as an example, that ends with the line: "And which is more, you will be a _____, my son/daughter."

The Lament of the Frog Prince

Ladder Set A

A1. Answers will vary, however students should create a timeline similar to the following:

1	2	3	4	5
Frog was in pond enjoying the scent of flowers, sound of waves, feel of wind.	Princess kisses the frog and turned him into a prince.	The prince went home with the princess and they were married.	The prince now listens to violins, smells perfume, hears laughter, as he attends the parties.	The prince wishes he were just a frog again.

A2. Answers will vary, but students should create a fishbone diagram listing "Kiss" as the cause, and several effects. Examples of effects include the following: frog turned into prince, frog married princess, frog is unhappy.

A3. The short-term consequences were the pleasure of the kiss and turning into a prince. The long-term effects were the loss of being a frog and all that went with it. The prince is sad for his loss. This is supported by several phrases from the story including: "If I had only known I was trading my whole world for the pleasure of a single kiss." Students may also cite other lines as evidence.

Ladder Set C

C1. Answers will vary but may include:

Metaphor	Meaning
glittering fire of diamonds	the sparkle of diamonds in the light
screech of violins	music
whisper of a breeze	a soft breeze blowing

C2. The prince is unhappy. Students may use the last stanza of the poem as evidence.

C3. Students will choose a different fairy tale to tell from a different character's point of view. They will compose a poem telling the story from the different point of view.

The Road Not Taken

Ladder Set A

A1. Answers may vary, but students should create a timeline similar to the following:

1	2	3	4
A man was walking down a path.	The path came to a fork.	The man took the less traveled fork.	The man had a good life.

A2. Answer will vary, but may include:

Cause	Effect
two paths	stood looking
many people on the path	worn path
few people on the path	less worn path
took the road less traveled	that made all the difference

A3. Answers will vary, but students might infer that the author was happy about his choice.

Ladder Set C

C1. Answers will vary, but could include: traveler, adventurous.

C2. Answers will vary, but could include: Traveler: "I could not travel both and be one traveler." Adventurous: "Then too the other . . . because it was grassy and wanted wear."

C3. Answers will vary, but students should state a concept such as "Following the less traveled path results in happiness and a contented life."

Sinking Sunset

Ladder Set A

A1.

1	2	3	4	5
At sunset time a boat is bobbing on the water.	The rotten timber on the boat breaks away.	The boat breaks apart and sinks.	The person on board the boat screams then drowns.	All that is left of the boat is a single timber.

A2. Answers will vary, but may include:

Cause: the timber is rotten and bobbing up and down

Effect: the board breaks

Cause: the board breaks

Effect: the boat falls apart

Cause: the boat falls apart

Effect: the boat sinks

Cause: the boat sinks

Effect: the person goes into the water

Cause: the person goes into the water (without a lifejacket)

Effect: the person drowns

Cause: the person and boat sink out of sight

Effect: the water is calm again

A3. Answers will vary. Students should use one effect from their answers for Activity A2 and create a fishbone/cause and effect graphic showing the cause and as many effects as they can.

Ladder Set C

C1. Repetition: up and down; rises and falls; splash; falls; screaming; sinking; nothingness
Onomatopoeia: splash

C2. The character drowns and dies. Students should use phrases from the poem to prove this fact. They are to write a paragraph, using their proofs, to support this idea.

C3. Answers will vary. Students should write one or more paragraphs comparing the title of the poem to the events of the poem. They should explore the connections between the two.

Sunset

Ladder Set B

B1. Answers will vary, but may include:

- the clouds turn gold and purple
- mountaintops glow
- hills turn red
- the sky turns pink
- shadows fall
- tired men come home
- the moon comes out
- the stars come out
- the night birds sing
- the wind blows

B2. Answers will vary. Students should categorize their answers from Activity B1, then give each group a title. Categories included: colors, sounds, sights.

B3. Answers will vary. Students should create two generalizations about sunset. Example: The sky changes during sunset.

Ladder Set C

C1. Answers will vary, but may include:
Metaphor: crests are glowing; hills are dyed
Simile: like shadowy, fleecy shrouds
Personification: air seems blushing; the moon will show her pale sad face; stars as her attendants

C2. Answers will vary, but students should note that the author likes the sunset time of day. Evidence would include the facts that all of the descriptions are given using positive adjectives: gorgeous, glorious, wondrous.

C3. Answers will vary. Students should create an original poem titled "Dawn." The poem should be modeled after "Sunset."

The Visit

Ladder Set A

A1. Answers may vary but should be similar to the following:

1	2	3	4	5	6	7	8
He gets up.	He gets dressed in his best clothes.	He shaves.	He gets out his coins he has saved and put them in a brown sack.	He takes the sack and his keys and gets into his truck.	He drives to the city, to the prison.	He parks in the lot and takes the bag of change to his grandson.	He visits his grand-son in prison.

A2. Answers will vary, but students should use a graphic organizer (such as the fishbone) to show cause and effect in the poem. Some examples: cause: needs to shave; effect: lathers face.

A3. Students should recognize that the grandson is in jail/prison. Evidence should be cited such as chained links, barbed wire, and behind the paned glass.

Ladder Set B

B1. Answers will vary. Students should use details from the poem to create the list that could include the following: old, careful, slow, considerate, kind.

B2. Answers will vary. Students should categorize the answers from Activity B1 and title each group. Categories may include age, caring, and personality.

B3. Answers will vary. Students should create two generalizations about the old man and use details from the poem to support the generalizations. A generalization could be: "As people age, they move slowly and carefully."

A Winter Morning

Ladder Set A

A1.

- snowflakes falling
- frost-covered glass
- wind
- pumpkins replaced by evergreens
- snuggle under downy comforters
- warmth of their beds
- chill of the room
- cold ears
- fires crackle
- bare trees sleep
- winter has returned

A2. Answers will vary. Students should create ways to group the answers from Activity A1 and create a title for each group. Example titles could be: sights, sounds, feelings

A3. Answers will vary. Students should make at least one generalization about each group from Activity A2. Example: Snow and frost indicate that it is winter.

Ladder Set B

B1. Answers will vary, but may include:

- dressed royally
- sleek golden handbells
- performers
- singing
- dancing

B2. Students should classify their answers from Activity A1. Examples could include: music, dance, theater.

B3. Students should make generalizations about art across generations/culture/time. Example: People use art in their everyday lives.

Nonfiction Answer Set

These are suggested answers only. Answers will vary.

Economics 101

Ladder Set A

A1. Bartering, using beads as "money," using lumps of different metals as money, pressing metals into rudimentary coins, printing paper money.

A2. Answers will vary. Ensure students are supporting their answers with evidence from the text. Possible answers might include the following: Prices for goods would be uncontrollable because there would be no competition; supply and demand would not work because the producers, not the consumers, would be setting the prices; and so forth.

A3. Answers will vary. Ensure students support their answers. One possible answer is that the implications are that the consumers, or the citizens of America, are really in control of the economy rather than the government and/or the corporations that produce goods and services.

Ladder Set D

D1. Answers will vary. Students' answers should describe the evolution of money without using the same words and/or phrases as the text.

D2. Answers will vary. Students should include the main components of the economy such as trade, goods and services, producers and consumers, and free enterprise. They may also include monopolies.

D3. Answers will vary. Check students' drawings for details and accuracy.

Mass, Density, and Volume

Ladder Set C

C1. Answers will vary. Possible answers might include the following: creative, genius, scientific mastermind, observant, a little bit crazy, eccentric, and a loyal subject to the king.

C2. Answers will vary. Possible answers might include the following: You must know the mass and volume of an object to determine density; they all pertain to how an object exists within space; and density is always related to mass and volume, but mass and volume are not always related to each other.

C3. Answers will vary. Students' answers should recognize that legends are often meant to teach us lessons. In this case, the lesson may be that science can determine the truth of a suspected crime. Perhaps Archimedes was the first forensic scientist.

Ladder Set D

D1. Answers will vary. Students' answers should describe the difference between mass and weight without using the same words and/or phrases as the text. Mass is how much matter is present. Weight includes mass and gravitational pull.

D2. Answers will vary. Students should include the main components of the legend such as the suspected gold theft, the task given to Archimedes, his discovery of water displacement, and, perhaps, yelling "Eureka!"

D3. Answers will vary. Check students' word problems for details and accuracy.

Population Explosion: How Math Helps You Understand America's Past

Ladder Set A

A1. Virginia, New York, Massachusetts, New Hampshire, Maryland, Connecticut, Rhode Island, North Carolina, South Carolina, Delaware (NC, SC, and DE in 1638—these three can be in any order), New Jersey, Pennsylvania, Georgia

A2. Answers will vary. Possible answers include: Math is instrumental in determining the immigration numbers and the population numbers and in determining the percentage of immigrants of each nationality when the Immigration Act of 1924 was passed.

A3. Answers will vary. Check students' answers for supporting evidence from the text, consistency of point of view, and accuracy of representation.

Ladder Set D

D1. Answers will vary. Students' explanations should accurately represent the data presented in the graph without merely listing it. Answers may reflect the following: in 1790 the most citizens lived in Virginia and the least lived in Delaware.

D2. Answers will vary. Students should include supporting details from the text. Students' answers should also be consistent with supporting or not supporting the validity of the subtitle.

D3. Answers will vary. Check students' answers for originality and accuracy of details.

The Systems of the Human Body: Part I

Ladder Set B

B1. Answers will vary. Check students' lists to ensure they include legitimate examples of body parts.

B2. Answers will vary. Students should group details into logical categories without using a miscellaneous or other category. The categories should be correctly labeled as close to or far from the heart.

B3. Answers will vary. Generalizations should be broad, overarching statements about the importance of blood to the circulatory system.

Ladder Set D

D1. Answers will vary. Students should restate the quotation in their own words and not merely make minor changes to the statement. For example, a possible response might be: "The lungs are the largest organs in your chest, but the left lung is smaller because it shares space with the heart."

D2. Answers will vary. Students should include the important elements of inhaling, such as expanding lungs, passing through the trachea and bronchi, red blood cells picking up oxygen and dropping off carbon dioxide, and the diaphragm contracting and expanding.

D3. Answers will vary. Check students' answers for originality and accuracy of details.

The Systems of the Human Body: Part II

Ladder Set A

A1. You swallow food; it enters the esophagus; it enters the stomach; the stomach muscles move it around while the stomach produces acids and enzymes; the acids and enzymes turn food into a semiliquid paste; the paste travels to the small intestines; nutrients are absorbed into the bloodstream; leftovers move on to the large intestine; the water is removed; the solid waste collects at the rectum; feces leaves the body during a bowel movement.

A2. The stomach begins producing acids and enzymes; the stomach muscles are activated to help move the food around.

A3. Answers will vary. Students should mention that if the gastrointestinal system was not functioning properly that their bodies would not be able to absorb much needed nutrients, would not be able to rid itself of waste, and so forth.

Ladder Set C

C1. Answers will vary. Students should describe how the neurological system controls the messages that are sent within the brain and throughout the nerves of the body. They should clearly show how these actions are similar to a control and communications center.

C2. Answers will vary. Possible answers might include: Without nerves, arms would not know where to move, hands would not know what to pick up, feet would not know where to walk, we would not feel pain, we would not be able to see or smell, and so forth.

C3. Answers will vary. Check students' answers for justification with relevant supporting details and appropriate alternate title.

What Is Sound?

Ladder Set B

B1. Answers will vary. Check students' lists to ensure they include only examples of sounds. Lists may include the following: voices, shouting, whispers, computer humming, music.

B2. Answers will vary. Students should group details into logical categories without using a miscellaneous or other category. Example categories could include the following: human noises, sounds from mechanical machines.

B3. Answers will vary. Generalizations should be broad, overarching statements about sound. An example could be: "Human voices make many different sounds."

Ladder Set C

C1. Answers will vary. Students should clearly describe how sound works in terms that a deaf person can understand. Most answers will likely focus on vibrations and waves.

C2. Answers will vary. One possible answer is that the closer together molecules are, the easier it will be for compression and rarefaction to occur because the molecules do not have to travel as far to collect together and they cannot bounce too far apart.

C3. Answers will vary. Check students' answers for justification with relevant supporting details. Also ensure that students' answers are not longer than one sentence. Phrases are acceptable.